7-50

CH00481312

A Hastings Fishermen's Museum Publication

Voices from the Hastings Stade

The museum would like to thank the interviewees involved for their co-operation and time, without which this book would not have been possible.

Edited by Peter Broughton, Jeni Bryson, Nona Jackson, Paul Ornsby & Philip Ornsby

This first edition published in January 2012 by:

Hastings Fishermen's Museum Publishing, Rock-a-Nore Road, Hastings, East Sussex, TN34 3DW
Telephone: 01424 461446
Email: hastingsfishermensmuseum@ohps.org.uk

The Hastings Fishermen's Museum is administered by:
Old Hastings Preservation Society (Charity No. 221623)

ISBN: 978-0-9571444-0-8

Printed in England by:
Impression IT, 2 Maunsell Road, St Leonards-on-Sea, East Sussex, TN38 9NL
Telephone: 01424 852116
Website: www.impressionit.co.uk

Acknowledgements:
© Portrait Photos Simon Hookey (Subject Photographs)
Other Photographs supplied by interviewees or sourced from museum archive.

Front Cover Image:
May 1966 - Fishing boats on the Hastings Stade with flags at half mast due to the death of Bunk Harffey fisherman and Chair of the Winkle Club.

CONTENTS

INTRODUCTION

This booklet was made possible by means of a grant from Renaissance South East under the headline title "Different Stories: New Perspectives" allowing the Museum to embark on an Oral History Project. Initially our team, Phil Ornsby and Peter Broughton, spent two days at Brighton Museum getting advice on recording equipment and recording techniques from Kate Richardson (Curator of Oral Histories).

This was then followed by further training at the British Library, where time was spent learning more about the art of interviewing from Rob Perks, Curator for Oral History at the Library. Here we were able to conduct our first "mock interviews" using the methodology learned from the talks given. We were then asked to demonstrate the Museums' work in a workshop conducted at "The Lightbox" in Woking. We are also indebted to the Stade Education Project overseen by Beatrice Rapley which provided the funds for the continuation of the project.

We have now conducted interviews with many of the people involved in the Hastings fishing industry. These include current and ex fishermen, fish salesmen and the fish market auctioneer and we want to continue to expand our collection and understanding. This is a very time consuming project particularly when doing verbatim transcriptions of the interviews. Locals know that the fishermen have an accent and vocabulary that is unlike any other and this has to be conveyed in the written transcription.

Of course the only way that the richness and vocabulary can be appreciated is by listening directly. In order to give the booklet continuity we have had to carry out some editing but this has been kept to the minimum possible.

Charlie 'Perkins' Adams

5ᵗʰ of July 1930

Family History

I was born on the 5ᵗʰ of July 1930 at 19 Woods Passage in All Saints Street. I went to the little All Saints School, the infants school first then up to what we called the big All Saints in Clive Vale and then onto Clive Vale School, where I left when I was thirteen in 1943.

I was going to the beach when I was going to school. The teacher wanted some herring took up to show the class what herring looked like. So I went down on the beach at three o'clock in the morning. At first I couldn't get out of the house because a policeman was standing outside having a smoke by the light, so I popped back in and I come down the side entrance, down Swaines Passage, down All Saints Street out on to the beach.

My father was going in the 'Boy Billy' then with Ned Muggridge, they was in partnership and I heard him say to my father "Look out Perkins got some trouble coming here" I was only a little chap then. He said "What's that?" and Ned said "Charlie's coming over here." and me old man, he looked at me and said "Whatever you doing over here at this time of the morning?" I said "I've come down because I want to take some herring to school!"

War Memories

We spent our childhood here in the war, always got a little bit of fish if we could out in the boats, a bit of pocket money and that, but in the war we were evacuated just before they dropped all the bombs in All Saints Street. Seven dropped down through the Old Town and we got away just before that we went down to Somerset and we was in Chard in Somerset, just outside of Taunton. Didn't enjoy it there, well the people weren't no good. We went into a major's house down there and we thought we was going to have a nice meal, when they took the big silver top off it was just a sausage underneath it.

I had two sisters, one's alive now and one has died. We all went down to Chard and me uncle Fred was there too, Didhea Beeney, all of them. We all went down together and I had to go to school. The first one that piped up to say something when I arrived was Derek Ryder, they said "This little fella's just come from Hastings does anybody know 'im?" and Derek shouted, "Chaaarlieeee!!!". I think he was glad to see me.

We weren't there long, a couple of months, no time at all. We came home because we didn't want to stop there; we came home on our own backs. When we got to Hastings there was a warning on, it was in the evening. When we came out the station we had to walk all up over the West Hill and come down that way to get up to Tackleway, because you weren't allowed along the front that time of day as there were soldiers there with the barricades up.

At the time to get onto the beach you got a pass at fourteen years old. The pass would let you onto the beach because all the tank traps were up, guards both ends and you had to go to the police to get a pass, show the pass, go down on the beach. That was at sunrise to sunset, then you had to be off the beach.

We used to help them with this and that, earnt a few shillings if we could because it didn't cost a lot to live those days you know. We was happy anyhow, very happy. I do remember the doodlebug and planes and that you know, but really we was too happy looking after ourselves I think, being young and growing up you know.

The Mayflower

When I was old enough I went straight into fishing, I've never done anything else

From Left to Right: Charlie 'Perkins' Adams Senior, Steve Adams, Bill Adams, and the children are a young Charlie 'Perkins' Adams and June Adams in front of RX289 'Mayflower'.

but fishing. My father was a fisherman before me and I liked it so that was it. I went fishing with him on the 'Mayflower' first; he bought her in the late twenties. She was built in 1913 for the herring catching, but she never came out, she wasn't finished in time. Her first trip to sea was in 1914 out on the Diamond, twenty odd miles out. So she was about twenty year old when he bought her, he was in partnership with the 'Boy Billy' at the time.

I believe Billy 'Kid' Phillips crewed her with Teddy Phillips, his brother, and of course Alf Pepper went. His father went to sea helping him and he also said at that time, because he always liked a good meal, that he could do a good bit of cooking; he said he was the best hand that he had with him, Alf Pepper.

I was thirteen when I went regular with dad. I remember putting on me new sea boots, we had to send away for them because I only took a five, and then they was too long on the legs for me where I was so short. I went down by the Dolphin on the first day, the winch sheds were where the net sheds are now. The bottom one, southern side, our shed was right outside of there and I went walking over onto the beach and a nail went up through me brand new boots and tore the side out of them; I never did wear them to sea!

It was pretty dangerous fishing in the war, but there weren't so many mines an' that about then, they had cleared a lot of the mines out of it then. But I was unfortunate to see one body on the water, which we tried to pick up; old Jim Lang was along with me father then and Walter Head, I more or less took his place. Anyhow this body was on the water and we think it might have been an American as he had a light bluish uniform on, and we tried to pick him up, but he was just a skeleton, you know. Old Jim said to my father, he said, "No let him lay, let it be his grave."

We caught a bomb up there at Harley Shute once; we were in the little boat 'Little Paul' that we had built. The trawl hadn't been down not ten minutes and she started hanging up you know, slowing right down, and when we got it out the bomb was in it. Father wanted to drop it back down and I said, "No! Don't let it drop in case it does blow up!" Because there's no water up there you know, very shallow water, so we ended up towing it down to the harbour here. All the boats an' that going at night time all had to stop because they blocked the harbour up, wouldn't

The 'Little Paul' RX88 now exhibited at Brighton's Fishermen's Museum.

let anyone come in and out the harbour. That was 1959 I think. The army disposal team, which we phoned up, came down and detonated the cordite on the beach. I think we got fifteen, I don't know if it's shillings or pounds for the damage we'd done to the trawl!

My father retired from fishing about 1960 and I carried on single handed then, out all the time with her. Then in 1963 I had the boat decked in, had the deck put on the top of the 'Little Paul'. She's at Brighton Museum now.

'Perkins'

When my father was a little kiddie nobody had ever heard him speak, nobody, and the family thought they had a 'duffer'. That's the way they spoke that time of day and they said 'I dunno what we're gonna do with him if he can't speak'.

This one evening they ended up at the pictures, his mum and dad and that, and they see a picture. At home several weeks later, they were sitting down talking about the film that they'd seen, and they said, "I can't remember the butler's name in that film. Can anybody remember that then?" Everyone said "No, we can't remember it." Of course the little chappie piped up and said, "PERKINS!" and that's where he got his nickname from, they named him Perkins Adams.

Packing Up

I packed up in '81 or '82, I pulled all the tendons in me arm and that, and I couldn't lift any weight or anything with it and I had to pack up. Oh it was like cutting your arm off. You're lost, when you've been to sea all your life, you can't live without it, that's all you know, you have to do it, you know. I had to stop, the hospital said "It's up to you" but I couldn't work on me own and even with a crew would only be working with one arm.

I've always lived in the Old Town, I was born in 19 Woods Passage then we lived in 32 All Saints Street just below Woods Passage, then we moved up to 26 Tackleway, and then after that, in the war, me father bought 11 Tackleway and before we got into it they dropped a bomb up near the lift and it blowed all the bay windows out of our house and we had all scaffolding up with red lights when we went down to live in it. I got married in 1974. Up till me wife died four years ago I lived in

Gladstone Terrace, lived round Gladstone Terrace and we bought the house there in Collier Road in '75 and I've been there ever since.

Fishing Now and Then

I've always been trawling, I done a little bit of herring catching an' all like that but I was trawling and messing about hooking years ago, land lines and lug lines an' that you know, hooking but apart from that we've always been trawler men you know. Fished all through the year, sometimes went to Newhaven, yep we went there, sometimes go up Eastbourne fishing, up Langley yeah, then we come home from there, when we were at Newhaven we stopped in the harbour, had a fortnight round there then come back home again you know. Well we had little cabin bunks down below, makes your back very sore, not very comfortable, not at all like a feather bed.

We only went as far down as Dungeness and back and I have been fishing down as far as Shoreham one night we went right the way down there, from Newhaven that was. Well there wasn't much of the fish up at Newhaven and we went right down by Brighton, right the way down, there but haven't been down there since you know, we only got down there once.

Well, fishing today really to us it would be a joy ride, you know, with all the modern gear and all of that, course when we had to do it then you just had to push the boats about and that, break your back; there it is you had to do it, push the boats out and everything but now when it's all modern and that I mean it's far easier now than it was then.

I would say there's more fish about now. Well it's just the same in Rye Bay you see it's always noted for plaice coming out there say in January or February sometime they come early sometimes they come late; sometimes there's a lot one year and sometimes there isn't half as much and that's that. No, they always reckon, years ago, that if you had a gale east at Christmas time and that then you get more plaice coming in the bay, well it comes down through. But whether that's true or not I don't know. And another thing with all the brood and that out there is only a feeding ground all the little brood if you go shrimping in the winter time or shrimp trawling a perishing cold easterly wind you'll see all those little teeny plaice, little penny stamps but when the wind's southwest or mild you won't see any of them. Now why's that? That's strange in'it? Don't know whether scientists today know or not. Maybe they should pick the fishermen's brains, it wouldn't take long to pick

RX126 'The Clupidea' - The first vessel with an elliptic stern built in Hastings.

them! Still you never know do you.

I wish I'd never had to pack up; I didn't want to pack up from the sea, never. I'd have gone on for ever, well till I couldn't do it anymore, you know, and now I feel I'd like to go back now, I would. If I was fit enough it would be okay, but just couldn't do it that's all, I'm a bit too old now I think. Graham Coglan is 70 now and he still goes out a bit. The oldest two what I knew when I was going to sea was Alec and Eric Eddy Mills in Rye. One was 81 Bob was 79 and they had hand cats then to winch the gear up they did.

Well when I was fishing I knew the Bartons, "Kestrel", Alfie Barton, that's Dennis' brother, Ned Adams there, Jimmys' uncle, "Wintry" what we called him, Old Croxer was about then, all that lot," Quiddy" Mitchell, George Simmons, Jack Simmons. Tom Adams, you know, Jimmy Tollers' father, all them, Junk Gallup, Teddy Terrell.

I never fished with them; I'd only been in The Mayflower for some time, with me father, yep and me father, they learnt all their fishing and know how not with their father, not with me grandfather, they all went to see blimming old Cusher Timms they did, all the boys did, but there's only the three boys that took up fishing, you know.

My grandfather he was fishing all his life, he had the 'Clupidae': She was the first elliptic stern boat to be built at Hastings she was. Well the saying is that years ago there was two brothers come over from France but whether this is true I don't know. It's only what I hear from people, you know. They came over from France, one stayed here and one went up into Manchester and that's where we originated from. All the family were fishermen: in Manchester today we still have relatives.

We did take one of the relatives Adams to sea with us and when he come on aboard

Charlie 'Perkins' Adams.

with us, it was on a Sunday, it turned out he was a Parson!! He blessed the sea because he was spewing all day long! Then when he come ashore he had cheek enough to say "I have enjoyed that." Cor blimey.

Taking The Family To Sea

When I was going to get married, she [Charlie's niece] wanted to go and have a trip with me, I said well it'd be early, you know, in the morning but I went called her up and that, then she come, everybody on the West Hill knew she was going to sea before she come down here, she was telling everybody and that. We went to sea, and we had a nice day but I put the railing gear over the side but she was railing nearly all day for mackerel, she never had anything you know, never caught nothing, and then when I went over there she was half asleep sitting there on the top rail sitting on the deck with her hands over the top rail trying to, funny I said, "What you got on here then!! Look!" I said. "You've got a mackerel on here!" and when it come up it was like a little pipe cleaner. And she had to take it home to show her aunt and it was nearly cooked by the time she got home, in her hand.

Oh what a mess she was in when we went over, 'cause she came to sea trawling one day, we had a good day trawling, you know and all the cuttle fish was about then, so of course pretty little girl and that all her clothes, everything was as black as a rook. We only used to catch them by accident then we used to break their necks and chuck 'em away. Only as a rule, as they come up in the trawl, they go after the other fish. They nearly always go for the best fish either sole or plaice or anything like that. Then they start sucking that, taking everything, all the goodness out of it you know. That's why you get hold of 'em bout the top rail when the head on and kill 'em, have to do so many of them.

Rules And Regulations

I remember that years ago all the boats from here and Rye went round to Newhaven and blocked the harbour up there. All anchored in the harbour when they couldn't use the harbour because trying to ban the beam trawls that one. That was around 1975. Well, they were all beaming and that have so many jinglers and that on them you know. So much weight when you tow. Well they was all beaming nearly everywhere all the foreign boats was here you know we hadn't been beaming not much here. They beamed before the war an' that, but it was only like fishing that

Fishermen at the Newhaven Blockade 1975.

time then to what they was doing later, you know. They had four, five rows of jinglers on the trawl, big chains, heavy chain. They used to cut the ground up. They come from all round there, Eastbourne come there and everything, blocked the harbour up and we managed to get away from it that evening, 'cause my niece was with me and she had to go to school and that the next day and she had to be home you know and we were lucky enough to get away: us and Bertie White an' that. We got back home but the others stopped there all night they did. Whether there's any good come of it I don't know, but seems that if they get over that they can do what they wanna do, don't they.

Well with the French, they never did come in with the international law about the size of mesh and that, they still use undersize mesh to what we do, always have done. Everything that comes aboard with head and a tail they take. One time of day they had children aboard of 'em working with 'em what come out of the hostels and that you know.

The quotas were nothing on at that time of day, nothing at all, only the size of fish what was on then. Oh yeah the fishery officer used to check mesh size. They could be crafty about that you know, we was fishing in Newhaven at the time and Boniface and his deputy come aboard the boat but they sit down on the top rail on top of the trawl see him put his finger in and measure it with his finger and that but ours was all well it was always all okay. And also it was on a Friday night there was only us and Wintry went out on Friday night round there but Saturday morning when he sold fish, Boniface and them was there to see that you never had undersize fish on the market at Brighton.

Well, Boniface was a decent fella, well that's what they say but it was a nice job what he had anyhow, but we used to go up his house sometimes and we'd have a shower and have a wash and clean up before we come home he said "I've had to do it and I know what it's like," he said, "to sleep rough aboard a boat," he said "You feel lousy." Boniface and Chesters and all them round here worked from Eastbourne they did.

JIMMY 'TOLLER' ADAMS
2ⁿᵈ of May 1931

Family History

I was born on the 2nd of May 1931, 2 Crown Cottages, Crown Lane, Hastings, right behind the Crown Inn. My father was Tom Adams and my mother was Dorothy.

I had two brothers and one sister, the youngest one died when he was nine. It was 1943, during the war, he got a nail through his foot on the market, my Mother bathed it, but before we knew what had happened it had spread right through his body. Within three months he was dead, because you didn't have drugs in the war like we've have nowadays.

War Memories

I remember when the war actually started; I was eight and a half. My dad was called up straight away, because he was in the Royal Navy Reserve, like a lot of fishermen at the time. He had been in the Navy RNR for twenty years and my Uncle Ned was in it too. Dad was first called up in 1938 because of a scare, and in 1939 when the war started, away he went. At the time my grandmother had brought up a chap called Tommy Saunders, he went along too.

From left; Charlie 'Perkins' Adams, Jimmy 'Toller' Adams and Dick Harffey.

When they all got called up and volunteered in 1940, Uncle Ned, Henry, all the lot, the boat went over to Rye and laid over there quite a while see. Uncle Ned owned the 'Industry' when he got called up, but Frawsy White was took the boat in the war and around 1941 Fred Adams and Steve Adams asked my granddad if they could bring the boat back from Rye where it laid up the Strand, my dad was still away, so they used the boat until he got invalided out and came home in 1942, he'd been torpedoed twice.

They were very lucky really because just after that in 1943 the 'Boy Billy' got blown up with by a mine. There was also the 'EVG' in 1942, she almost got blown up by a mine, but she got away with it, because it blew under the sea, but on the 'Boy Billy' all three of them were killed. The only thing they found of one of them, trawled up a few weeks later, was a foot in a boot and that's how they knew who it belonged to, because he had white boots; that's all they found of them.

My dad wasn't far from them that day, but a year later my dad was out in Rye bay trawling and when your trawling the boat stops, when you got up under the headline, what you call the headline of the trawl and there was a mine coming up underneath the bottom. They were lucky enough to see it, because you can't always see things when the water is very dark. So they see this mines horns coming up, and dad cuts the trawl away, saying to my brother, who was with him and Jimmy

Helsdown, 'Put the engine in gear as fast as you can because if that goes up under us we're going up with it when it hits the bottom'. Lucky enough Rye bay is mainly mud, consequently it settled in the mud, and they got away with it. They went and told the other boats and they all came home, and of course the coastguard who sent the minesweepers up from Dover. They blew up sixteen mines in Rye Bay that day. Another thing that happened in the war was the bomb that hit the Swan in 1943, it hit the back of our house first and ricochet like that, it knocked the back of our wall down and then went into the Swan.

The 'EVG'

Well 1942, the spring of 1942, they was out Trawling and one of the fighter planes was coming over and machine gunned the 'EVG', and a cannon shell hit Jimmy 'Grizzle' in the stomach and blowed him, well nearly in half really but of course she caught fire and Quiddy and Georgie 'Nunkum' they brought the boat home and she was dished up, didn't take long, but if she was dished up she was caught fire on all her side 'an all that.

Then she went out, I don't know exactly when, I thought it was '42, anyhow they was out there trawling, there was Quiddy, Georgie 'Nunkum' and Pepper was the third hand, and a mine went up. Either the otter board hit the mine or the headline or the ground rope hit the mine and up she, went and blew the bottom out and 'Junky' Gallop who wasn't too far away. He was in a boat called the 'Oritava' and he slipped his gear which was then picked-up later, and picked all three of 'em up. But Mr Pepper had a gold watch hanging on the mast case and he went to go down below and 'Quiddy' said, "Don't you bloody fool you'll go down with her." That's how fast she went down 'cause the bottom was blown right out. But anyhow they got away with that, and that's as much as we know about that.

Fishing in the War

I was fourteen when the war finished and I was at All Saints School in Clive Vale, but it was in 1944 when I first went fishing with my dad. You see in the war, most of them were all old boys over the beach, because the rest were away fighting and consequently us kids used to help the boats up. When you got to be about twelve years old, they'd let you have a pass to get through the barbed wire and help the boats up. We'd get a box of fish off the boats and go and sell it for three and six pence then, big boxes, well two and a half stone.

They caught mostly plaice and soles. Not so many soles though, because you couldn't go night fishing during the war, no way. Consequently mainly plaice, dabs, all that sort of thing, but there were stacks of fish if you could go off. My Uncle Ned had two hundred and twelve stone, in one day, which was daylight to dark in the wintertime.

That happened even though there were loads of boats out there, at Rye, even all the big Newhaven boats were down here fishing. One was called the 'Little Old Lady', another, the 'Boy Eric', and the 'Harry H Leach'. Those boats were about seventy feet long and they fished out of Rye when they could. Rye is a very tidal harbour you see and they could go all the way back to Newhaven after, as they only needed to have one big haul down here and they could go back with two or three hundred stone.

The first boat I fished on was the 'Boy Bob', I was around fourteen, it was my Granddads boat then, Granddad Adams, and it was in Rye. Then in 1949 I joined the Navy, we were called up in those days, National Service. I was on a cruiser and we went all around the Med, all round the place. Actually it was a good job, you had to do your two years, but then I had to do three more years after that in the reserve.

I was in the RNSR, Royal Navy Special Reserve, because I'd done a full gunnery course aboard ship, up to four inch guns and small arms up to four inches; Bofors, Oerlikons, Pom-Poms. I was on a Pom-Pom aboard the cruiser 'Superb', she was registered at eight thousand, but her actual weight was nine and a half thousand, she was similar to the 'Belfast', same armament with six-inch guns aboard her

I enjoyed it, but I wanted to get home. See my dad had bought a boat while I was away. There was a bloke called 'Tiny' Breeds who had two boats on the beach, the 'Edward and Mary' and the 'Leading Star' which was the boat my dad bought. He knew that when I came out of the Navy there wasn't going to be enough room for three of us on one boat, so he brought the 'Leading Star' for when I came out even though it didn't actually work that way, but anyhow, that was his idea. He had bought the winch and everything and in the end he had three boats 'Leading Star', 'Boy Bob' and 'The Dove'. 'The Dove' was a nice boat actually, beautiful.

When I first came out of the Navy I went on the 'Boy Bob' at first, because Dougie White and old Charlie Geering went out in the 'Leading Star' while I was away.

Tom 'Toller' Adams, Jimmy 'Toller' Adams' Grandfather repairing the nets in 1914.

When they'd finished I went in it with Dougie White, she was getting a bit old then and so my dad sold her to a school teacher. After that I went in the 'Golden Spray' with 'Ginger' Moon, that was around 1950-51. She belonged to T.A. Fish Salesman, and had a diesel in her; we only had petrol paraffin engines. We were trawling all the time. I've been in so many different boats it's unbelievable.

Another one I went in was the 'Surprise' with Dickie Joy, we went mackerel catching all the summer. She had a twelve horsepower in her and was another one of T.A.'s boats; he had several, the 'Enterprise', a lot of them. In the war he had about five or six boats going to sea, I can't think the names of all of them, but he had loads of punts going to sea as well, he was a fish sales man see.

We mainly fished in Rye Bay at the time, but it all depended see. You would go to Rye Bay in wintertime because that was where the fish was, but as you came up to March, April, all the fish come inshore and consequently you would follow the fish. Sometimes you'd be only five minutes off here and then you shoot the trawl.
You never got cods then like you do now, even though in the war they got plenty of cods, but just after they just seemed to go missing, they just went, we didn't hardly see a cod. The only place you might get them was on the Hooks Hard and we never

fished there because you would lose your cod end, but there wasn't cods then like there are now.

Probably because all those big trawlers came back, in the war they all went as mine sweepers and after the war they all came back into commission, but they had all this modern gear, so they started mopping them up. But now see, with fishing dying down a little bit, the cods are there and breeding fast, even if we've got quotas that say you can't sell them and can't catch them.

The Fog

I've been nearly run under twice in the fog. The first time I went out with three other boats down through the hole, what we called the 'hole in the sand' and the 'hole in the trail', it's about five and a half miles off of Hastings. I worked my way down there and worked my way back, the other three went the other way, including my brother who was alive then. I pulled my trawl up with fourteen stune in it and did only one haul, but I kept out there for three hauls.

I shot on the fourth haul, the others weren't there then, they'd come ashore with two, three stun. That's how it goes; those that were on the White Land and on the harbour came home, because there was no fish there. At that time my Uncle Henry looked after me, we use to call him 'Mad Henry', as he was mad as a March hare, used to get drunk, not like the rest of us of course! Anyhow I've stayed there and just on my last haul, it came thick as a hedge with fog, anyhow I'm west part of the hole and I hear this steamer blowing. I had a bell aboard her so I got it standing up and I was ringing it has hard as I could, I could hear this steamer blowing in the distance, sounding like he is quite away. I still standing there ringing and I don't hear him for quite a while, then all of a sudden he blows his foghorn and it was a bloody big tanker! I nearly jumped over the side because he was so close.

I could actually see him in the fog he was so close; actually he must have seen me because he blew his foghorn. I got the trawl up as fast as I could and came away. My Uncle Henry was my boy ashore then, he came down to the beach and it's coming on dark now, so when I come ashore he asks 'where the hell have you been?', he says that all the rest of the boats come home heading. He thought I didn't have any fish like the other three boats, but I did. I had forty stune, of fish.

Twice I've hit rocks coming home, coming in this thick fog this day, when the ebb tide takes you up this way. Rather be up this way than down there under the cliff I thought, next thing you know there is a bloody great rock looming up out of her. I spun her round but still hit it and the boat glanced off. I didn't know far I was, but I kept going, and there again is another rock sticking out of the water, could have been the castle rocks for all I know, I wasn't sure where I was. Then I hear this banging on the shore and guess where I was, Glyne Gap! The ebb tide had taken me up there.

Anyway I steamed out and fell in with Charlie Perkins, who is my cousin, 'How about Charlie', I asked him, 'Where about are we?' and we were off the end of the houses, anyhow I shot the trawl and we both pulled down here and we came ashore.

Another curious time was when I was coming up in the morning once. We seemed to have more fog then than we do now, and we didn't have any radar or nothing, no echo sounder. So I'm pulling in this morning and I know I'm getting into shore because I'm watching the otter, watching my gear coming up in the shallows. When I had a look I was getting right the way in somewhere, nearly ashore and guess where I was! Right up in Fairlight Glen. I thought it was good that I'd got the trawl up because there wasn't much water under her bottom. I got steam up and came ashore.

You'd be surprised how the fog was then, one day I nearly hit the pier coming up, I couldn't see anything. The pier loomed up like a bloody great cliff when I nearly hit it that day.

'Toller'

Different parts of the family have different nicknames; there are the 'Toller' Adams, 'Goff' Adams, 'Perkins' Adams and the 'Nunkum' Adams. There were a lot of other Adams too, but they're not related to our family, probably going back years ago, like the fish salesman Adams, they weren't any relation.

My mother was an Edmunds, she was one of eleven kids, the middle one of them. They had several lots of twins like they have now, like Michael and Jimmy who both have twins.
Before the war, in the twenties and thirties, my Granddad Edmunds used to do a bit of drifting along the shore, but in the summer time he'd work on the bathing station.

The Bathing Station

That was where all the bathers used to be nude along Rock-a-Nore, men one side, women the other. That's true, I'm not messing about, I used to be along there, I went along the bathing station for four years. Dickie Joy and Doug White were along there too, bloody good job, we had catamarans and used to sit on top.

At that time me and Dickie Joy had the 'Surprise' and all we use to go up and shoot a few pots at Warrior Square at the same time, the boat would only have laid there anyway, it belong to T.A he didn't mind, see T.A was like that.

The thing is you wouldn't earn a copper if you went pleasure boating now. At Eastbourne they still do it in a big way, but that's Allchorns, they have their own boats but I think they're even finding it a bit of a pinch now. People don't need that sort of thing now, you don't get the visitors you use to, used to be thousands of people on the beach in my time.

When you used to come down the road from the railway station, there used to be thousands of people get off the trains and they just used to go down straight onto the beach. They'd even used to put special trains on just for the days out. You don't see that anymore. When I was along on the pier station, they had a band on a Sunday, army bands and all that playing and the pier would be crowded people listening. That was only in the fifties and sixties. People all go abroad now, they don't worry about it anymore, you wouldn't see a soul along there if there was a band there now, you wouldn't see a soul.

'The Favourite'

The first boat I owned was 'The Favourite' once belonging to Dickie Adams. She was a big punt with a Ricardo and a six. I was only young and I lacked judgement, ignorance right, and I thought I'm not messing about so I bought her for one hundred and eighty pounds, which was a lot of money in 1951. The thing was the engine wasn't a lot of good, Ricardo, it was a poor type of engine, they weren't top rate and they'd break down a lot.

One day we got into trouble and we were towed home by the lifeboat and so consequently I brought a diesel off of T.A., the same fish salesman which owned the 'Golden Spray'. I brought it off them for one hundred quid and thought I'd done all right. She had a big engine case you see, so we put half hundred weight on the top because of the vibrations. Then when we'd gone to sea this half hundred weight fell down through the top and smashed one of the filters. So after all that we had to be towed home again! We had the other six-horse power going and Quiddy Michell towed us in so far to the harbour. I had it all mended, but it didn't cost too much, but I still thought I've had enough of this, so I sold it back to Bovril.

Now big Bovril was a businessman, he was my mum's brother and he bought 'The Favourite' off of me for about £140. At the time they were pulling the Palace Pier down and he used it to earn a lot of money, because they were scrapping it, and he had all the divers and that onboard of it. He did all right out of that, sometimes you're part of history aren't you.

They said at the time it was an accident that the Palace Pier burnt down, I don't know how it could have been, being derelict. In the war they blew the piers in half, because it could have been used as a landing stage for the Germans. So there was a

Jimmy 'Toller' Adams.

big hole in the middle, they rebuilt some of them but they didn't do that one, and it somehow it catches fire? How it did no one ever seemed to know, a mystery, must have been the blokes who owned it, perhaps it was an insurance job. Anyway they were pulling the lot down and up until a few years ago you see parts of it sticking out of the sand, up near the Victoria Hotel.

After that I went and worked in London for a little while. That's where I fell in with Renee Cresswell, Mark Gardner's mother, I came back home again pretty quick, I couldn't stay up there, I came back here to go fishing. But I used to go up and see her and in the end they moved down here.

That was around 1955. They first came down here on holiday and they stayed with my mother and us in Crown Cottages. She liked it so much down here they wanted to buy a house, but her father was still alive then and they lived in her father's house up in Enfield, Middlesex. I was going to buy a boat then, but she wanted to get a house. I did buy a boat in 1958 because they didn't come down here until the early sixties because the old man was still alive. When the old man died, they sold the house and I put a deposit down for a house up on Croft Road, it had about ten rooms in it, £2400 pounds we paid for that in about 1964. I put £240 pounds down for a deposit, a lot of money in that day and age, anyhow I loaned it to her, and they moved down here and she paid me off.

Mark came to sea with me for a bit when he was a kid. He used to come down fairly often, but one night he and his mate came with me and they had a frightening time. The weather looked to be fine, anyhow by midnight it gave an imminent gale o' wind: that was the night when Joe Martin got his medal.

The lifeboat wen' off and we came ashore at four o'clock that morning, blowing a lot of wind, but there were four boats still off from Hastings and this one Rye. His name was John Morris, I knew him quite well, his father worked for the Smith's, the people on the station. His father was one of the directors on there he had a big house up Fairlight. Anyhow instead of going to Rye waiting for the tide, what he done was keep steaming westerly and he'd ended up off Bexhill. We could all get ashore, but she was a harbour boat, so he couldn't stick her ashore here, so they called the lifeboat. I went home and went to bed about four o'clock, five o'clock that morning; it had started raining and blowing hard, really blowing.

So Joe Martin got called out and got a medal for it, a lot of us said "he got a bloody medal, but us lot was off there in the middle of the night too." Anyhow they took the crew off, they were three amateurs, John Morris didn't know anything and the two blokes that was with him were anglers, but they were trawling you see. They didn't know what they were doing, anyway he was a toff, spoke posh and everything, but he was a nice bloke to talk to.

The next day, she laid out there, the boat, she'd survived, they put the anchor down on her, the 'Simon Peter' that was the name of her. Stanley Pepper came up and towed her into Rye as a salvage op, she was a fibreglass boat you see, that's why I had a fibreglass one built after that, she'd stuck it out in a gale of wind that boat.

Engines

When I went with my dad we had a 13 and a 6: that was the Kelvins they were all petrol paraffin there weren't no diesel on the beach then at all. All the big punts had a 12 horse power Kelvin and all the small punts had a 6 horse power like we've got in the shed, but consequence is they got too expensive to run plus they never had the amount of power, 'cause I mean 13 and 6 you're getting one similar in a diesel got more power than them lot there, consequence is when they started getting the Lister's, Harold Pepper, Perkins and all them had a 22 Lister he had to put in the Enterprise. Harold Pepper had a 22 horse power put into the Enterprise: a Lister Blackstone that'd be in the '50's they was the first ones, but John Gladwish had a new boat, the 'Jessie', 1947 but he had a Lister Blackstone put in there first time, he had one in there when it was brand new, first built. Also George Steel had a massive big engine. You couldn't start it by hand, you had to have batteries, consequence is if the batteries run down you've 'ad it!

During the First World War the fishermen didn't trust them 'cause they could never turn them on. Several of them blowed up because you had the cornices up through the seacock, well 'course they forgot to turn the pipes on. When you start the engine consequence is water comes up, you start it on petrol and when it's hot turn her over to paraffin because they couldn't start them on paraffin it was too cold, consequence is they forget to turn the water on because they was frightened of 'em and several of the engines blowed up, they was frightened to have 'em. And the 'Edward and Mary' had a Gleniffer, they done the same with that they forgot to turn the water pipes on to run the heat to cool 'em off, 'cause they were new to engines and frightened of 'em, consequence is that one blow up. The plugs went up under the deck she blowed up!

RX53 'Dorothy Melinda' coming ashore.

They didn't know about engines and they had to learn about engines, they also had a problem with thinking that the boats might not be able to be strong enough as some of the big boats only had a 6 horse power when they were first in them and they had the 12 horse but then it went on to 13's 'cause the 13 had a massive big flywheel, used to stand up on the flywheel, we had a 'dog' on the front of the flywheel used to put the hand in, turn it like that and when it's just started you had a wheel-nut on it that turned it quick and that picked the engine up but it also had air on the side had a primer full of petrol put it on the air intake and that would help start it and away they go. And you kept them on paraffin for about two or three minutes 'til they got a bit warm then they would go over to petrol; you had to do that again sometimes even when it was warm you had to put on the starter. You had a little tank, about four foot on the side of the boat with petrol; that went down to one part of the carburettor, 'course a 13, like the one big carburettor, 'course she only had two plugs but they had a bigger version of that, a 26 Kelvin which had four plugs but they was very expensive to run and they were big engines but they were so expensive.

In time the value of the engine outweighed the worry that they had about the engine and they saw that they were working so they accepted them. They had magnetos on the side of them see and when you come up some of them boats the decks used to leak and the water used go into the magneto and they used to cut out even with the trawls down when they've got the trawls aboard if they leaked down, through the deck as a lot of them did as they were getting the fish, 'cause all the water comes aboard with the fish if it went down on top of the engine it would spark the engine off and she'd stop and you had to be careful 'cause if you just shot the trawl again and the engine stopped you got all that gear back up again 'cause the drive came back over the top of it.

So in time then they would use the same engine that they were using to drive the boat to haul the nets, that blowed the capstan: used to have a belt that would come down on the front and you had a flange on the front of the big flywheel and they had a flange sticking out, the belt go down on there and we used to have a clip called Octopus 27, you get the belt and put them together that's Octopus 27 and on there on the deck you had a handle with a jockey wheel on it to pull that belt tight and slack it off, when it slacked off, it only needed a little bit of strain on it and it'd stop, sometimes they just go around very steady but when you put any strain on it you pull the jockey wheel up, that'd tighten the belt on the flywheel that got more strain on you could put more strain on the capstan.

Slum Clearance

The clearance in the Old Town to make way for the Bourne took place in the '30's but the actual road wasn't built through there until 1959, '60. I was 14 when the war finished and they knocked all the houses down before that and they just left it. It was very different when I was a child: there was two breweries up the Bourne, one was Watneys and the other was Breeds brewery, well Breeds one of the last ones brewing the beer up there, as you come down through the Bourne there's a bloody great big brick wall which we used as a playground for kids because there was stumps in the road stopping cars coming up there, you could only push a cart up through there, because up through Uckfields, which was an engineering place up High Street and their back entrance was in the Bourne which went straight through. That's where they had the blacksmith's shed. When we wanted any work done we used to take it up on the cart: me and my dad we had a big keel made for the 'Boy Bob' 1946, we went up with the cart with all the metal and all this sort of thing and the blacksmith'd make it and get 'em to bring it back down the beach and had it fitted, you see.

When the war came, they started building the flats, the first two blocks of flats as you see them at the bottom of the Bourne was built just before the war and it just started building the third lot which is just past, you know where the little grocers shop, well they just started building one lot there when the war started and all the bits was left there the whole time because everything stopped when the war started. You had a massive big tank put there in case of fire from bombs and all that sort of thing. You had a big concrete tank about nearly as big as this room for fire in the war and that was laying in that space now where them houses are. That's what we call the Creek, as you come down from there that's what we call a Creek from All Saints Street down into the Bourne 'cause there's a river runs down there see. The people were rehoused and moved away to Bembrook some up the top of High Street, just past the church: in 1937 most of them. Lot of 'em went to Clive Vale; they build them on that side of Clive Vale between 1935 and 1937. They moved all them people out of their old houses in fact some of them got compensation and some didn't, whatever compensation you got was very, very small 'cause they knocked them houses right down, 'cause it was a slum clearance, see. It was called a slum clearance but isn't it a bit strange that the slum clearance should be exactly where they wanted to put the road. Them plans were there before the war like I told you, they wanted to build a road right through here, knock all the sheds down 1937 and the fishermen beat them and took them to court.

That was Sidney Little, he was going to build a road right through as far as Pett. He was going to shape the cliff down like that on a slope and build a road on stilts all the way along there, that was his plans but gawd knows where he thought the money'd come from. He'd just built the front there, Bottle Alley the swimming pool, all that lot he built, all that lot along the front, all that new lot. Well he wanted to keep going along the front here but then the war started and then everything stopped dead so that was the end of that but then after the war he was still about, Sidney Little, he was the Town Borough Engineer and he put the plans through for that road, he made all the plans for that road but I don't think he foresee it as it was, he was getting an old man then I don't know what year he did die but he was getting on, then I think it was a different borough engineer, I think a bloke named Baxter took it over. Sidney Little is well known because of all the stuff he did down the underground car park and with Bottle Alley and all that. Trouble is the war came: you used to have all lights underneath there it was a beautiful place, shutters when the wind was blowing and all this along there but of course when the war come everything laid there for six years and the army took a lot of that over in the war, especially in the underground car park used to train all the soldiers, have 'em marching up and down inside there see: Marine Court was full of RAF personnel, most of the hotels was full of Canadian soldiers, all their lorries along Bottle Alley and all that would be underneath now all the way along.

They were against the changes in the Old Town but they got better houses, but it's too far away along Bembrook but they couldn't alter it because they got no houses to live in. We lived in, and I was born in Crown Cottages right behind the Crown, that never come in the scheme, They wan't new houses they were built 1888 but they was new to what some of the others was, what was pulled right down.

But the ones in Bembrook were built in about 1935 to '37 to take the people whose houses had been cleared. Biddy Stonham wen' up there, Weasel, Wilfie's old man, they all went up there then, Will Martin, they all lived up there, lot of 'em lived up Bembrook but it was so far to walk but as soon as they could get out of there they transferred down to Hastings Wall, a lot of 'em as soon as they could get out of Bembrook 'cause it was too far to walk from there if you had to go to sea early in the morning, there was a lot of 'em in the latter years, I would say, that transferred into Hastings Wall. That's why some of their families live there now: behind the London Trader, Hastings Wall.

We had a big building up there called Scrivens Buildings which was built in 1888. Most people went in there but you had outside toilets and you had to share toilets.

It's all been pulled down since, all reinforced concrete but it was down Crown lane where the new houses on the right hand side, that's where Scrivens Building was. Big building, we lived in there 'til I was seven, I was born in Crown Cottages and then we moved over to there. I would imagine you'd get twenty families or more, in there. They knocked them into one place, let's put it this way, they modernised them: you had to share toilets. In the latter years two flats were made into one, right, it was two flats, one there and one there and they share toilets but in latter years there was only two like a bedroom and a kitchen and another bedroom like two beds and the kitchen that's all some of 'em had. Well about ten years before they pulled 'em down they made them into bigger places altogether; they had their own toilets but they was outside toilets and they made them more bigger altogether so people had more .

I had two brothers and one sister and we lived in Scrivens Building but we only had a small one. We moved out there before the war, my mother did, 1938. Yeah, you see what happened we lived in Crown Cottages, I was born there but my uncle and auntie, they had half the house, my mum and dad had the other half, right, but when they had me they moved out right, we went up Scrivens Buildings then after that I had another brother after that, my Charlie, so then we moved down into All Saints Street. I think altogether, we lived in five houses in all down All Saints Street.

'Dorothy Melinda' being 'christened' by Jimmy 'Toller' Adams after being positioned outside the new train station in 2008.

PETER ADAMS

11th of December 1951

Family History

I was born in Hastings in a private nursing home, Fernbank, on the 11th of December 1951. I started off at the Convent in Old London Road, but the nuns quickly realised I was a bit of a handful for them, and then went to West St. Leonards for two or three years and then ended up at Hastings Secondary School for Boys, commonly known as Priory Road. At seventeen and a half I joined the Air Force and I was in the Air Force for seventeen years and then I worked abroad for another four years, and then decided to come home when dad was taken ill and I didn't want to see the business, auctioneers and wholesalers, go out of the family.

My great grandfather decided that it was more lucrative to sell fish than catch it, so back in 1897, he gave up fishing and became the auctioneer for Hastings and we carried on being the auctioneers till 2005 when I packed up the auctioneer: so there's four generations of auctioneers; my great grandfather, my grandfather (he had half a dozen boats during the war) and my father in the early days of him being the auctioneer had boats but when the 'Pioneer' went down with all three of the crew he decided that boat owning wasn't for him. My father would never talk about it but I think they went aground in fog and the boat smashed up on the rocks and of course the crew just drowned. It wasn't long after that that he sold his other three boats: 'Breadwinner', the 'Endeavour' and the 'Valiant' both which

RX90 'The Valiant' coming ashore after collision in which George Mitchell lost his life.

were red, which was quite unusual on Hastings beach, they were completely red. Most of the wooden fleet was built after the war, the 'Valiant' was built in the late forties. She is that awful shape because my Dad gave the builders in Newhaven the dimensions he wanted: he wanted a very strong boat. Anyway they phoned up and my uncle answered the phone and dad had wanted twenty six foot on the keel, (I can't remember the exact figure) and Uncle Bill said, "No it's twenty six foot overall", and that's why she's such a short boat and the ribs inside are about six inches apart, because dad said he wanted so many ribs in a twenty six foot boat on the keel but it makes it an interesting boat to look at and very strong, and it survived that collision in the Channel but 'cause she's so short, rolls like a pig. There was a collision out in the Channel and somebody was killed. I think probably, it was after dad had got rid of her, and I was in the Air Force then so I only sort of got basic information. I've got some pictures in the Lifeboat House about it.

Dad was born and bred in Hastings, lived in Hastings all his life other than the war years. Dad being ex navy, he was always very cautious anyway, but after the

'Pioneer' the boats had to be absolutely perfect, and it just wasn't lucrative to do it because there was no money in it 'cause the cost of keeping these boats on the water. He wouldn't stint on servicing, the engines were stripped down every year and it became an expensive pastime. Where, locally of course, people go until the engines break down and then they fix them, but dad wouldn't, couldn't do that because after losing three crew members he just couldn't do it any more.

The crew still got paid the old way with a share, the usual thing, a share for the skipper, a share for the crew, share for the boat, and a share for the gear. It was share in four and a quarter shares. So, if the boat earnt, £4.25, there would be a pound for the boat, pound for the gear, pound for the skipper, pound for the crew, and twenty five pence for the boy ashore. Well he got three shares then crew got one share and dad's maxim was, any skipper worth his salt, owns his own boat and I think that still rings true. He had a very good skipper in Brian Stent and of course Brian being a good skipper, went off and bought his own boat, it's still on the beach now, RX60. The only person that probably is not true about is David 'Spider' Peters who's never owned his own boat but was always a good skipper, and caught a lot of fish but he never wanted to own his own boat: didn't want the responsibility of a boat. RX59, 'Our Lady' was owned by a film star and the skipper, won't mention any names, but the skipper that took it was, was useless and so the boat never earnt any money. It should have done, it was a beautiful boat, well found and no money ever spared on it for gear. It always had the best of everything, but the guy was not a good fisherman 'cause if he was a good fisherman, especially in the fifties when The White Fish Authority was giving interest free loans to buy boats. Anybody worth their salt would buy a boat.

I came out the Air Force and I had no intention of coming back to Hastings other than for visiting family and holiday; maybe retire in Hastings so when I left the Air Force I went and worked in Oman for a year, and then I got a job running a power station in Libya for three years, the contract had finished but then I just got another contract, to the Great Man River which was the irrigation of the Sahara. It was Gaddafi's idea to bore for water and irrigate the Sahara. I'd got a commissioning job on that for pumping stations, which, is still going on now, so it was a long term job but dad had had a heart incident and he said would I come before I went back to Libya and see him. He made an offer and I thought "Yeah, why not." so that's when I came back to it. I was enjoying Libya: it's not the horrible place they say it is, it's actually a nice place to work. I enjoyed that but then I came home, dad was coming to the end of his industry career. I think he was 63 when I came home, just coming on to 64 and I thought "Well this has been in our family nearly a hundred years, it would be foolish to let it go." so that's when I turned down the job in Libya and stayed in England and the rest is history as they say.

As a business we didn't own any boats, and then a lovely steel boat called 'Hannah Louise' I think or the 'Louise', but out of Rye, pulled up on the beach here, lovely, it was forward cabin and before there were any steel boats at Hastings and she was pulled up on the beach, for whatever reason and I heard the guy was in trouble and wanted to sell her, and I made him an offer, but it obviously wasn't high enough so I didn't get into boats. I certainly was interested; I was in the financial situation, I could afford to buy a boat. I had a crew lined up but the guy wouldn't accept my offer. That was when I came out of the Air Force. I'd been the auctioneer back in Hastings probably three or four years then and I thought going back into boat owning might be a good thing.

Fishmarkets and Auctions

The new market came into being at the end of the eighties, early nineties. The council approached users of the market saying it was losing money, they didn't want to have to be responsible for it anymore and could we see a way forward. So the FPS (Fishermen Protection Society) with the guise of Paul Joy, myself and my partner Barry Connolly and Bud White, who was treasurer of the FPS at the time, we got together and we formed a limited company to take over the running of Hastings fish market, which was the initial thing. We called it Hastings Fishmarket Enterprises just in case there was any surplus money and we could spend it on other things other than fishmarkets and that's how it started. Then the EU came out with several draft of how fishmarkets should be and look in the future and when it got to draft four they said this was the final draft, and this was what would be the future of fish markets. With this in mind, Paul Joy and I went up to Scarborough to see their draft for fishmarkets with an architect that we had asked to have a look at designing for us, Ralph Wood of the firm Wood and Royal, and being an Old Town guy and very much into preservation we thought he would be a good person to have on board to design. So we looked at Scarborough Market and then came back, had a feasibility study done by the Sea Fish Industry Authority, who came up with a plan that under EU draft four for fishmarkets, all fish within the South East, that would be from Portsmouth to the Thames, would have to be paper handled through Hastings i.e. it couldn't be moved, it had to have a certificate from the main port; the main market for the South East was gonna be Portsmouth right up to North Thames coast, so everything landed within there would have to have a certificate

Far Right: Joe Adams, Peter's father, standing beside Wally Hoad in the Winkle Suit at carnival time.

issued by us to be sold on and to be moved. It was planned to charge two or three pence a kilo for this certificate, and we would have had somebody sit there with a fax machine, issuing these certificates. It was a license to print money. So therefore, this was the Seafish Industry Authorities, the amount of income the market would make would be phenomenal. So we went ahead, we got a MAFF grant for half of the building. The council loaned us the money, they said it was a gift and we would have to repay it as the notional interest on the loan. So the ground rent was going to be thirty seven and a half thousand pounds a year, which, with the Seafish Industries business plan we would be paying easily and more. Unfortunately, the paper work and everything for having a regional fish market never materialised, so that income never came along. When we built it interest rates were 15% so the notional interest was, on this notional loan was thirty seven and a half thousand. We're now down to half percent and so the council are arguing, "Well, it never was, it was always interest," and so we are in discussion with the council, we have really from day one have always been in discussion with the council. We have never met this interest payment/rent because the whole premise of building the building was the business plan of the SIFA, on us being the controlling market for the whole of the South East. So we now have a fishmarket that handles the local boats, plus a few from away and not doing anything that it was designed, or the business plan funding, because they never come on stream.

Some boats come from away to here, that was part of the agreement, because previously, there was all hell to pay when Brian Stent left my dad and bought his own boat and decided to fish out of Rye, and dad was selling his fish in Hastings and there was absolute riots and all the fishermen were in there saying to my dad "You will not sell his fish, we don't want that black fish out of Rye. You either sell all of our fish or you sell his. We'll all stop selling through you if you sell the Rye fish". That's how strong the sentiment was in Hastings, that Hastings fish was sold in Hastings market. Poor old Brian was left to sell his fish wherever he could, but he did alright out of it, but it's now part of agreement with the new market, the council stress, that anybody who wanted to land fish at Hastings market had to be allowed to. The only stipulation that the FPS made was that the Hastings fishermen would pay 1% of their income for ice and their fish going through the market, and

Second from left: Peter Adams holding a Dutch auction at Hastings Fish Market.

away boats would pay 2%. And that is the only difference to the system. The system now is, the local boats now pay 1.5% and away boats pay 2%.

The original market, I'm led to believe, is next door to what is now the Bamboo House, before that was the Harbour Restaurant, and that used to be the hexagonal market. That closed down and then it moved, over the other side of the road where I have pictures of my grandfather, (who died in '48), on that market, that was a corrugated one where the Playland is now, next to the boating lake. Then in the early fifties, the new market was built by the council and that's when my father moved in to the current site, and we knocked that down in 1993 and built the new market that stands there now. I took over doing the auction when my father retired at the end of '85.

It was a Dutch auction: for those that don't understand a Dutch auction, you start high and you go down until the fear in the eyes of the people that are desperate for the fish will pay more for the fish rather than bidding up: it's a system that sounds strange but actually works very well. Certainly in my father's day, when a lot of the small plaice went to Birds Eye for processing, he'd come down and there was a price that was the Birds Eye price and he would say, "That's it, no more fish to sell, all going to Birds Eye!" so the system worked quite well. Hastings boats only, 42, 44 I think at the most, all brought it on to Hastings market and dad sold for all of them but there was no boats outside of Hastings that were allowed on the market. They brought them ashore then they would ice it up and put the fish there through the day and then at five o'clock next morning we'd have the auction. The boy ashore for each boat would put the boxes of fish through the scale, the auctioneer, me and my dad, would look at it, look at the size and the quality and sort of set the high price. Sometimes you'd get what they called snapped, which meant somebody jumped on your first price, 'cause they knew there wasn't a lot of turbots or something like that on the market, and they would jump. But normally you knew that people were going to snap, so you'd start high anyway, so it was a better way of getting a good price. Shops would come to buy mostly.

Hastings now has four fish shops, but back in the sixties there was two Macfisheries, there was another one in Robertson Street, there was one in Bohemia, one in Silverhill. There was probably about ten or a dozen fish shops in Hastings in those days, plus Eastbourne, we used to buy and sell, send fish to Eastbourne, you know, especially turbots and dover soles, and large plaice. Bexhill had about five fish shops and then there was probably something like half a dozen barrows and twenty or thirty, forty vans going out as well. The vans, the hawkers would buy local fish directly from the auction but they would go to Billingsgate for the more exotic stuff that wasn't caught in Hastings. I used to get a company called Greenslade up from Poole. They would come up from Poole two or three times a week, especially during the dover sole season. Littlehampton there was a company there, Shoreham and Brighton all had big companies who would come to Hastings to buy fish certain days. I would phone them in the evening and say, "There's a load of plaice here, a load of soles or cod." and they would come over, and buy next morning.

They changed it from the Dutch auction into what they do now because there had been problems: there was information coming out of Eastbourne and Brighton, mainly via Network Fisheries, saying that they were paying higher prices for fish than I was attaining on the auction. I went over to Network in Newhaven and said "How are you doing this?" and they would put together the slip and the tongue soles together as one size (we sold fish in four or five grades). Well if tongues were making say a pound a pound and slips were making two pound twenty they would average it out and say "Well we're paying one pound fifty." but of course the boats thought they were getting one pound fifty for their tongues, and they weren't you know, so there was some misdirection certainly from people who landed to Network who were talking to fishermen over here. Personally I think the people we had buying here, for soles, were actually fighting each other for soles and they were buying on spec and often, whatever anybody else says, often, some of these people would lose money buying soles, 'cause they were buying on yesterdays price, and if the price collapsed… Sometimes they got it right, they must do otherwise they wouldn't carry on doing it: I though quite often they got it wrong and lost a lot of money so, but in the end I personally think and I talk to a lot of the people who now agree that the auction, on the whole, was the best way of selling the fish.

Rye does it the same as what we do here but there's not the buyers now, this is the problem, there's not the volume. I mean I was selling to forty vans, there's about six or seven vans out of Hastings now, most of the shops have gone and the big buyers from away have closed up or are not interested: they're sourcing elsewhere, so you've lost that customer base to hold the price up, that's the problem. I think that, like Greenslade was coming from Poole, so we are talking, two hundred and fifty mile round trip. So you've got to buy a lot of fish and make reasonable money to be worth doing that trip. Now, I used to buy herrings and mackerel and sprats from him, which he'd bring up to me so it was a double trip. So that would help his costs, but unless he can fill that lorry up going back to and then sell it on for a profit, it was not viable for him, and transport costs have gone up and up.

I noticed the market running down as the sole catches dropped off, quite dramatically, and you could see an annual drop off of catches. I know a lot of the boats were, each year, to keep their income going, increase the amount of net they were putting in the water. When I first started I think two, three fleets was the norm: when I finished eighteen to twenty fleets, you know, and each fleet being a kilometre long was being shot and some of the boats were putting eighteen fleets in, doing nine fleets one day and nine fleets the next just to try and maintain their standard of living and the catches were still dropping off and it does coincide with the shingle bank dredging, whatever anybody says, you know, I saw that dropping off and I wrote a paper and some statistics for the ministry to show it, but it came to nothing. Dredging is dredging and shingle builds houses and roads and fuels the economy.

I retired from auctioneering four years ago this month, so that's 2005. By that time I was selling for about half the fleet which was about twelve, thirteen boats. The fleet had reduced to about mid twenties by then it coincided also with Network Fisheries, who were the people brought in to handle all the fish, when they decided they didn't want the auction. When this happened, about two thirds of the fleet went to Network. I wrote a letter, which wasn't taken very well by some members of the industry, saying that if anybody left and went to Network, that would be fine if they changed their mind within the first month I would take them back with no penalty, and after that if they came back month, two months, three months there would be a one percent increase in the commission. I got a difficult letter back saying that I couldn't do this, and it was detrimental to the industry. So it's all gone under the bridge now and at the end of it when Network went bankrupt they had about twelve boats and I had about twelve for the auction and when I did pack up I was down to about half a dozen then, and they really, I mean they all said would I still handle the fish, but I'd just had enough by then, half past one starts in the morning for twenty odd years, I just realised it's a good way of killing yourself getting up early six days a week like that.

Hastings was mentioned on Saturday kitchen for soles and mackerel, but in the same breath he also mentioned Alaskan salmon: now you know and I know that a little Inuit fishermen is not going out in canoes and catching this salmon, they're going out in huge great, (says it's much more ecologically friendly) trawlers catching these, and then they're being air freighted to England, so personally, I don't think that should be getting an MSC rating in Britain, because it's being air freighted in. That's my own feeling. I like MSC, (Marine Stewardship Council) I feel it can't do anything but good but I feel it's not cost effective for us to promote it, you know, as we say to our customers in the shop "This fish is MSC fish." just 'cause it's not tagged, it is caught by the same boats using the same nets, just I'm not willing to pay the registration fee for very little, I don't think there's a lot of feed back or help from MSC to the retailers.

Quotas

This is where I will be contentious: I am totally against quotas; I think it's a disgusting habit, chucking good fish back in the sea. I don't think any sane person can say that is the way to do it. The Icelandic, since the cod war, have managed their own stocks by closing the fishery completely, stopping anybody fishing in that area. They close an area and they do this on a daily basis, they watch what's being caught. The catches start to drop off and they close that fishery for three months, six months and allow spawning and rebuild and they have managed their fishery like that for the last eight years. They are allowed to go elsewhere, they still have a quota system, but it's not a dumping quota system, which is just ludicrous, throwing good food back in the sea to rot.

DEFRA have come up with a lottery type scheme for the excess quota allocations to go to the 'lucky' fisherman: if you win the lottery, fine, but then you're not: the girl that manages my shop for me, her father's just won the lottery and now half the beach aren't talking to him now 'cause they say it's not fair. He should catch that amount of quota, it's not that large an allotment he's got, he should catch it. I think he's got about half a ton 'til the end of the year. That's eighty stone; I mean you can get eighty stone of cod in one day out there on a good day so again it's the dogma of this is the quota, you can't do anything about it. They're not, like the Icelandic's, looking at it on a day to day, and week to week basis. The sea is full of cod out there at the moment. There should be some take of that and you should not be allowed to throw that back in the sea.

I was also a wholesaler, I was running both businesses and one of my best customers that I was wholesaling, this is away fish, filleted fish and exotics, farm bass and stuff like that, Tuna, all this sort. I was putting probably a third of my turnover into one shop in Hastings so I decided that when this guy was retiring it would be silly for me not to buy him out, because I would lose a third of my turnover so I bought him out. A girl had come to me who had been in the industry all her life, said she was keen to manage the shop and that's what I do now: She manages the shop and I do the administration accounting and stuff like that and cover holidays which I don't like: and I don't have to get up at one thirty in the morning!

Lifeboat

I got involved with the lifeboat through the family dynasty again in 1989. My father took over the lifeboat in the early fifties when he was the auctioneer and Chairman of the Fishermen's Club, and they didn't have an Honorary Station Secretary, and dad volunteered, as he was a lieutenant commander in the Navy during the war, and so ideally suited to taking over the lifeboat which he did in the early fifties, and he did 35 years as Honorary Secretary and then finished up as chairman of the local branch. I'd been home about two years then and I thought, one needs to put something, I know it sounds a bit pompous, but one needs to put something back into the community, when you're taking your living out of it, and so I volunteered to do it and I've been doing it for twenty years and one month now, so between us we had 55 years.

I'm still Honorary Secretary; well it's now the Lifeboat Operations Manager, same job, different name. The RNLI changed the name, I think primarily because we started to do a bit of inshore stuff with flood defensive: if you was to turn up at Uckfield when it flooded saying "Oh I'm the Hastings Lifeboat Honorary Secretary." it just sounds like you are a pen pusher. Lifeboat Operations Manager actually gives you a title that people outside the RNLI will actually understand. I'm in charge of Lifeboat operationally. If the Coastguards want the lifeboat to launch, they page me, I phone them, find out what the call is and then decide which boat to send, I have a couple of deputies as well but the boat is not allowed to be launched without a launching authority, which is me and my two deputies, without our say so and this is the system of the RNLI which I think works so well. If I've said the Lifeboat can go, and the coxswain thinks it's too rough, he can say, "I'm not going." He has the last word that way. So there's a check and balance. Two or three times the old coxswain, Charlie Sharrod and I have walked down the beach and had a look at it and said, "What do you think, I think it's okay?" and we go out. We've had a consultation about it but when push comes to shove, if I say it's not going the coxswain cannot have the last word and say yes it is. So it's a check and balance: if I say it can go and he says, "Well I'm actually not happy, it's not going." then he can refuse to go, but he can't countermand my order and say, "I am going."

When my father was doing it, all of them that were in the lifeboat were actually fishermen, every single crew member was a fisherman or ex fisherman. The mechanic at the time and the following mechanic were ex fishermen. Joe Martin, who ended up as coxswain mechanic, was crew for one of my dad's fishing boats, and even though he was losing a good skipper, my dad encouraged him to go into the lifeboat as a mechanic 'cause that was a full time job as such. When I started, Charlie Sharrod was a crew member, well his father was a fisherman, but he actually wasn't a fisherman, he was a BT engineer, Freddie White, 'Whacker' White, he was a crew member, Joe Martin was still coxswain and Dougie White was second coxswain. 'Podgy' Ball, Robert Ball, he was crew member, it's difficult to know when some came and some went. When I took over, I took over just as Dougie and Joe retired so Freddie White, 'Whacker', was made coxswain: I think he was called 'Whacker', because he'd 'whack' you if there was any trouble. He'd quite a fiery temper Freddy, he's a lovely guy and he's calmed down a bit now, but I think in his youth… So I think that's where it came from. Jason Adams has been on the crew, come and gone, Mark Ball, Richard Ball, another Ball on the crew several of them have come and gone you know but at the moment, the only fisherman is Richard Ball, the rest are all non-boat related. I think that happened because the RNLI has had to become extremely professional, certainly in the last seven or eight years. At one time we were very close to being shut down by the Maritime Coastguard Agency because of our training regime although regarded as the best there was, there was no record.

We have what's called now CABT, Confidence Based Training, and everybody has to be re-trained every three years and they have to keep this training up, and there's a constant re-training throughout the year. Virtually all coxswains now within the RNLI have what's called a RYA offshore yacht masters certificate and I think although the fishermen are all consummate seamen the technology overtook them and they got frightened. Too much technology, that and of course we got two chart plotters on the boat now though we carry paper charts they're not really needed, they are there for emergencies, because you've got a moving map of where you are, so local knowledge is not as desperately important as it used to be.

One fisherman I will mention, who stayed until he had to retire, is Micky Barrow. He was an excellent crew member, he was forced to retire at 55, (although the RNLI has recognised that people are getting fitter they have upped the age to sixty again.) Mick, he actually took the boat as coxswain when Freddy White left and we hadn't appointed a new coxswain and was instrumental in the rescue of a vessel called the 'Tern' which was a coaster that was sinking by the bow and with his knowledge of the beach managed to beach her in Bexhill on a sandy part, at low tide so she didn't sink. (Mick Barrow has been interviewed but not mentioned this story.) Well Mick wouldn't. He's too unassuming. There is a picture of the boat, you know, there was lots of pictures at the time of her drying out. There is a picture in the boat house of her. She is down by the head; a third of the way along the boat is under the water. We still managed to get her in. The engineer stayed on the boat and the master, everybody else got off, and we took them off, and then we escorted until Mick said, "there's no rocks there" and beached her on pure sand which is good fisherman local knowledge.

Joe Martin got his silver bravery award, and a fantastic rescue of 'Simon Peter' in force 11. Certainly 'Fairlight' she was only an eight knot boat, she was taking on water ballast, so the first two minutes of her in the water off the carriage quite dangerous when they're out in a force 11 with no ballast on the boat, the ballast drained out when she came ashore. Well it was an automatic thing but all because she got a ton and a half of ballast on board she was not the most stable of boats. Rolled like a pig in beam: any boat you know, boats like that, very similar shape to all the local fishing boats.

'Sealink Endeavour' The newest lifeboat came here just as I started. I was a deputy then and it had come in the summer and I started in the October so, but I remember 'Fairlight' coming. I was a St. Clements choirboy at the naming ceremony so I remember that well in the sixties. In 2009 we celebrated 150 years as an RNLI station. We got our old 'Fairlight' back, she's up on the Blackwater now. We brought her down by lorry and we had a good week of celebrations. We had to do a lot of work on her to get her up to scratch it's just a shame. When she left here, she was absolutely spotless. Joe Martin, the mechanic, always polished the floor, underneath the engines, 'cause his thing was if you've got a leak you can see where it's coming from straight away. The boat was spotless, always, you know, and some people may have unkind things to say about Joe, but he was a character, and he loved his lifeboat and he kept that boat in absolutely tip top condition.

JOHN BARROW

14ᵗʰ of September 1976

Family History

My name is John Richard Barrow. I was born in Hastings Old Town on the fourteenth of the ninth 1976. I lived in the Old Town at the time of birth in All Saints Street. Grown up all my life in the Old Town, moved away for a couple of years, but lot of people say, once you've lived in Hastings or born in Hastings, you can move away but you'll always come back, and yeah, absolutely love the place. Started at Dudley Road School and moved to All Saints and then up to Hillcrest and didn't really get on too well at school let's say, more interested in getting out and knocking around down the beach and making mates.

Well, when I left school, I messed around with the mates for a couple of years and then, well obviously always messed around down on the beach, but wanted to start earning some money. I started going to sea with Dad and had, six or seven years with him and really enjoyed it, and well, never really thought about doing anything else.

Fishing And Changes

Once I started fishing, that was it, that's what I was doing and that's what I was happy with, really loved it, quite a difficult job at times, but mostly in nice weather, nice job: Bad weather, not such a nice job, but you just take the rough with the smooth, but yeah really enjoyed the time I spent with him, but well, the way things have gone economically and things with Government quotas and well, necessity to pay bills really that's the main thing that has sadly led me to find employment elsewhere.

I'd really, really like to still be fishing on the beach, still come down every day and talk to the fishermen, and try an keep me hand in, do a bit, help dad out and stuff on the beach but unfortunately there's, money's not in it like it was before, and got bills to pay, and as I say I've had to go and find employment elsewhere. Which unfortunately leads me to driving a heavy goods vehicle round London most of the time. But I had to go where the money's at. I've still got a little boat, little canoe, mess around out there and just generally keep me hand into the beach, nice to keep on doing something really.

I didn't start until I was seventeen, I don't think, I'd had a couple of years just finding out what I wanted to do. Come down and worked till, well it was about twenty four, twenty five something like that and really enjoyed my time, but, wish I could do it now. I really miss it, I've got a dog and every morning take the dog for a walk, over the Hill and stuff. Obviously it looks out over all the boats and I just see 'em all steaming out every morning, and I wish I could be doing it, but I need guaranteed money.

Well, mainly the thing you catch in Winter is cods, and the government put a ban on completely catching cods which obviously if it's the only thing you've been catching it's the only thing you can sell. So, they've had to throw fish back, and well its just been a complete shambles really. So, if I'd have been working down there during, this winter especially, boys down there haven't earned anything for probably a couple of months. It's been bad weather and there's been no fish, I wouldn't have been able to pay bills, taxes and rent and stuff, it would have been impossible, so luckily really I have got other employment. But it does sadden me to have to leave it really.

So, I mean, I understand with the older fishermen that they've probably made their money in the past; they probably don't need as much money now as they did when they were younger.

I hang around the beach quite a bit, and I know a few of the young lads and they are struggling really, I mean a few of the bigger boys over here that have got the bigger boats they're obviously able to put more money into the fishing. Really when you put more in, you're obviously going to get more out, but with the younger lads, where they've got no money behind them, they'll find it hard to invest in the latest gear and the newest nets and obviously if you've not the really good stuff you're not going to catch the fish to pay the bills, so it's difficult.

Obviously where I was only a young'un knocking around, used to come down and help me old man out watch him help the other boats an' just generally see what's going on and it really struck me how much teamwork and how together the fishermen were. I mean they are now, but back then they had to be even more so 'cause obviously every one had to help each other out even more than nowadays.

Nowadays everyone's a little bit more independent but, back in the days before tractors it was a case of pushing the boats down the beach and really having to work as a team, making sure the boat stays on the wood. If the boat runs off the wood as you're pushing it down, have to heave it back up, someone have to go up the winch, start the winch again, pull the boat back up, get it back on to the wood, and yeah it's really good teamwork back then but nowadays everyone's a bit more independent, everyone does their own thing. It has changed a lot and I suppose it's changed for the good, it's made everything a bit easier.

The fishermen look after the other fishermen definitely, everyone knows that. If you're a fisherman you're part of a community and you're a hard worker and you're reliable, well most of us. Most people know if you been to sea then there isn't a lot you can't do, or there isn't a lot you're not willing to put your hand in to, don't mind a bit of hard work obviously. Out in all the elements, but yeah, there's definitely a team. I mean everyone over there loves the old man and it's a nice feeling, everyone always chats away to him and he gets on with everyone over there, and there's not a lot of rivalry between us, everyone seems to get on over there. Everyone's good at lending stuff, and borrowing stuff, some are not so good at returning stuff, but all in all a nice little community.

Dad has a good reputation, ever so good, well I suppose you treat people how you want to be treated yourself and when he first started down here, obviously only going on what people have told me and stuff, but he kept himself to himself, nice and quiet and helped other people out. Obviously been doing fishing all his life and wanted to start down here wanted to like branch out on his own sort of thing, and he came down here with quite a lot of knowledge to put into the fishing. Obviously didn't go round all big headed and everything, just done it all slowly and a few people asked him a few things about it and as he was a kid, grew up down here he knew where all the rocks were, all the ledges were and all the sand bars and everything which obviously helped him out; using the lobster pots in the rocks and the bass nets back of the rocks, but he's built a real nice reputation up for himself and he'd do anything for anyone and everyone seems to do everything for him so it's really nice yeah, he's done a lot, I mean it's given him a lot, fishing. It's given him, well it's given him his house, family and the kids and everything but also he's given a lot back to it as well, he's helped people out and he does a lot into research and he's been on a few committees and I think he's been on the committee here at the museum for quite a few years hasn't he? I'm not too quite sure how many the number is but he's certainly been on the committee for quite a while, but it's nice to think that you give something back and that's why I'm sitting here today. Thinking, helping and hoping that my little bit is contribution. I know the old man's made up with it so anything I can do to help I will.

I mean when I was fishing, I did it for six or seven years, there's only two or three times I can remember being, well, Dad'll probably tell you more but I can remember being banged out of bed a few times after too many beers the night before 'cause obviously when I was a kid I was doing it there was quite a lot of kids my age doing it. I mean we weren't earning great money not compared to what they was earning back in the day but we was earning good money for seventeen, eighteen year olds at the time, an' there was quite a few of us and one of the lads, Russell, God bless him, there's a tribute up to him down in the Church, in the museum, but we used to have a good tear up in the Old Town, it was good and there was probably a dozen lads sort of round my age, which made it nice. We had a good laugh, had a few beers with them but it was mainly in the afternoons. You'd go out, do your work in the mornings, get up four or five o'clock, go out, finish by midday, one o'clock, get in the pub, have three or four pints and you was back home by tea time, bit of dinner and to bed and that's how it went sort of thing. But there was a few times I didn't, I got banged out of bed I must admit, and few times I was pretty good at turning up on the whole shall we say, but I was pulled in a few times where I'd had too much the night before I must admit. But definitely really enjoyed it; some of the best days of my life spent at sea, definitely really nice good experience.

When it was cold, thinking about it really it's ah you wrap up pretty well. I mean if I'd had too much beer the night before I used to crash out down by the engine, where it's a bit warmer and I mean you wouldn't think someone could sleep next to an engine, banging up and down, getting soaked by the waves but you'd be surprised how well you can sleep, I mean for the first couple or three weeks I was quite sick most of the time, well, all the time; if it was calm I was alright but when it was a bit poxy, used to feel a bit ill, used to have the occasional spew. But after couple of weeks of it, that was it, used to go off in, well 'specially when we started bass drifting, used to go off in force four, five, sixes, and didn't used to bat an eyelid, an' if dad warn't concerned about the weather then I knew it was okay because he knows what he's talking about and it was fine with me. We had a few hair raising moments but that's what it's all about, improvisation an' when you're out there you've got to work as a team and know what the other persons doing, an' yeah it was a good team, and I really enjoyed it and I think the years of working with me dad brought us closer together. I mean I know a lot of people say they can't work with their parents and ruins their relationship but no. it's definitely. I mean Dad knew pretty much from the first day we went to sea that he wouldn't have to say it, if it was there to do, I'd do it without being told, and that's what a lot of it's about, common sense and using your loaf. If something looks like a hazard, doing something about it before it becomes a hazard or, well just generally just looking out for each other and yeah, its good, its good team work out there.

We started drifting for bass which was good and when we first started doing it, we did bring in some really good catches and I think one of the record catches for bass landed in one night on the market. I don't want to start quoting figures, actually I'm not too sure of the figures but its definitely one of the record lands of bass but the only trouble was, the only time you'd get the bass drifting is when the weather's not very nice and there's a bit of sea. 'Course all the time its calm the bass are on the bottom and in the rocks feeding. All the time the winds blowing it knocks the bass out of the rocks, sends them to the top and then you can catch them in the drift nets. But the only trouble is, you have to go when its not very nice and generally when its dark as well which you can imagine, on a little open top punt with a couple of lights, not really being able to see anything, it can get a bit scary But I knew if the old man says yes its alright I knew it was alright. But one evening we steamed out back of the harbour and as a backwash came from back of the harbour it created quite a big wave and as I looked round, the old mans looked at me and he says, well he says "You want to hold on to something here." and I could see in his face that he meant it and I've never seen that look on his face before and he was serious about you want to hold on, and as I looked around the boat I was almost looking down as we was going down this wave I was looking straight down the boat into the water. And I'm thinking that she's just going to carry on going and it's 'cause the sea that we was looking into must have been well twelve, thirteen foot tall and I'm thinking that its just not going to come back over the top of it, and she buried her nose into it and we took quite a lot of water on board. Luckily enough there wasn't that much round the engine and we just managed to get the pumps on and get the water out but yeah, seeing that look on dads face when he was proper serious, never seen that look before, you knew its going to be a bit of a rough ride. But, when I think of some of the things we've done. If Health and Safety was to have seen at the time they would have had a field day; well its all in the name of earning money and you never risked your life or anything stupid and you wouldn't intentionally put your life in danger, it's all about thinking about the situation and dealing with the situation before it occurs sort of thing, it's just making sure everything's all right. I mean we've had the engines stalled a lot of times and obviously the pumps only work on batteries and once the pumps have drained the batteries down, you're not starting the engine cause you drain the batteries with the pumps and when we've filled up with water a few times and have nets around the propeller a couple of times it's just a case of calling up one of your pals that's out with you and getting a tow home or at the last resort using the lifeboat; of course the others would take the mickey out of you, getting towed home by your mates! Generally I really did have a good experience thinking back on to some of the things we've done and some of the good times and some of the not so good times, but made a lot of good friends out of it.

Health and Safety

We don't get too much involved with the Health & Safety nonsense They've brought in everyone that goes to sea now must have a general first aid, general fire fighting, sea survival, just a basic knowledge of going to sea now. I mean, I don't think they enforce it really, I know people that go to sea and they haven't been on the courses, but been going to sea for twenty, thirty years anyway so they know what they are doing by now anyway. But it's a lot different to how it was, I mean they still can't police it, obviously there's been hands lost, people lost and people killed, but that's all part of it really, I mean I'm not saying you expect people to get killed but it's just one of them things that happens. I mean, if the health and safety was to come over the beach then the whole place would get shut down. People walk around the beach, there's notices up saying careful; wires, machinery, nets and all that but some of them boats that they pull up, if one of them wires was to part and someone walking up the beach, yeah, it don't bear thinking about, but that's all part of a working beach I suppose. And you take the risk but it's how safe you are, it's just using your common sense and not rushing around so much.

Friends Lost to the Sea

Steve Weatherall, one of my good mates, really, really nice lad, he couldn't do enough for ya, would help you out all the time; have a few beers with you in the evening, and everything, really, really nice lad, good family man and everything but I mean I suppose I'm a bit like him, I do everything hundred mile an hour, really you need to slow down and just take your time and make sure everything's all right. Steve went to sea one evening on his own, but never came back. They never found him, never found the boat, found a couple of fish boxes with his number on, but that was about it. That was, sadly, all that they found.

I don't really want to start quoting what's what, 'cause I'm not hundred percent sure on everything that happened, no one is. We think he was towing down off Beachy Head, there's a hell of a lot of tides that run down through there, and she wasn't the biggest boat, and if he had them hung up on something on the bottom. I mean I'm not an expert on trawling, but maybe if he had hung up on something on the bottom, and not been able to react in time it could have quite easily pulled the boat down. I mean, I'm only speculating, I don't know. All I know that he was an absolute top man and he would do anything for you, and unfortunately that's the way of the world it seems to be all the good ones get taken first and all the arseholes live forever, but sadly its part of the job. Maybe if there'd been two people there that night, maybe it wouldn't have happened, I mean, dad's sort of retired now, still keeps his hand in down the beach, still does a bit, but for the last couple of years, when I started working out of town, dad was going to sea on his own. I mean, there's a lot of difference between them, I mean dad's been doing it for donkeys years and he would only go and work two or three nets, two or three fleets, just like five or six hours, you know what I mean but he knows what he's doing: I'm not saying that Steve didn't know what he was doing, but Steve was there to earn money. Whereas Dad's just pottering around sort of thing. But, yeah, unfortunately some of the risks you take in fishing maybe sometimes, thinking back, shouldn't be taken. But when you've got a family and you're pushing to earn money, unfortunately it's there some of the risks maybe that get you in to trouble.

Russell was a really good pal, one of the best mates, really sad time, really upsetting time. I was at sea when it happened, and dad got called over the radio. It was one of our mates, Porky, and he informed us what had happened and well obviously Dad told us what was what and he didn't mess around. Me old man's not one to mess around with his words and he told me how it was and said "Look it don't look good. Russell's had an accident on the beach" told me what had happened, how the tractor had come back and crushed him between the boat and the tractor, that obviously, you know yourself if that happens he's not got much of a chance really, and that he was still alive at the time and they tried to do the best they could for him. We were well out back of the East hards, probably something like hour and half away. So we left what we was doing, come ashore but sadly by the time we got ashore he had died. No ones fault again. I mean it didn't happen at sea which didn't make any difference at all, he obviously still lost his life, but didn't put me off, no not at all, it didn't put me off. But, obviously makes you think, makes you think what ifs and all that but I mean he was an absolutely top lad, absolute diamond but he wouldn't have wanted you to leave the fishing, that's all he knew. I mean he was one of the best lads over here at the time, and it's just the way it goes again isn't it. It's always the good ones isn't it and life goes on, must look to the future.

Fishing Areas And Techniques

The hards, they're well just a rough set of rough ground runs up about three quarters of a mile off Hastings. The Hole well that's known as the hole a bit further out. I mean I'm not hundred percent au fait on all the distances and everything but you've got like top of the sands, you've got like fishing out on the banks and everything, where it all drops down. Where we only got a little open top boat, little punt, I mean we did go out like, ten mile, eight ten mile out sometimes which was mostly spent sleeping on the way out there and gutting the fish on the way back hopefully, but most of the time was spent in close working pots, lobster pots, eel traps, nets in the rocks.

Drifting for bass was seasonal, they tended to be eight, ten year ago never used to get them in the winter really 'cause maybe the water's warmed up. Maybe 'cause we haven't had so many cold winters, we seem to get them all year round now, which at the moment has been a godsend, because if you wasn't catching bass at the moment, well, I mean not really catching anything, but over the last couple of months, since the cod ban and stuffs been on if you hadn't been catching bass, selling bass you wouldn't have been catching nothing really, there's really a lot of soles and stuff round.

Fishing for bass usually when you shoot nets and leave nets usually, majority of the time you would shoot them East to West, you'd shoot them with the tide rather than across the tide and they would be fixed nets. They would be on the bottom with anchors and drag them down to the bottom with a lead line on and a cork line on so they hold the bottom and the corks bring them up say ten foot off the bottom. With the drifting you shoot the nets different: you shoot them from North to South, you shoot them across the tides and the lead line on 'em is a lot thinner and the cork line is a lot bigger so they actually float along the surface and obviously when the sea's rough the fish come up to the surface, either come to the surface to feed or come to the surface for protection, to save getting bashed around on the bottom and the nets drift along with the tide. In theory they stay from North to South and they just drift along and any small fish will swim through the meshes and you won't catch 'em but any of the fish that are sizeable you'll catch in the nets.

The one on the bottom, that's the static net, that's down there, that's what they call shoot and leave a trammel net or you get the sole nets, the nets without the wallings on the sides, which a lot of them are using. Well they're the same nets, they're just set up different: you can use either for either really, you can as long as its got enough corks on it and you take the anchors off you can use it for drifting or if you put anchors on 'em, more lead line along the bottom you can weigh 'em down and use 'em on the bottom. But the drift nets tend not to get too much damage, 'cause they obviously aint catching crabs or anything in the drift nets and if they're up off the bottom so you're not catching up on any rocks unless you're in too close but the drift nets tend to stay in much better condition than the nets on the bottom.

Really you can have as many nets as you can work really, in the time. I mean when we started off drifting we started off probably with twenty nets, something like that; talking about, oh probably about, three quarters of a mile, something like that and then sometimes you'd go off and you would get nothing in 'em and you'd get two or three fish in every net so the next time you'd use a few more nets and then try some different drift nets, and I think in the end we had about four miles of nets and by the time you'd finished shooting from the start to the time you finish shooting it was time to go and get the other end in and then obviously you'd just work the nets according to what conditions and according to what fish you're getting.

We never used the fish finder, I mean not when we was netting we never used to, we had one on the boat but occasionally we used it for mostly in close, finding rocks that had either covered, been uncovered by the sand, obviously with the tide it, you'd get ledges appear and disappear in close where all the sand shifts around and when you're using lobster pots its handy to know, I mean you can chuck the pot over the side and hold on to it and feel it bouncing along the sands and you can feel it when it hits a rock and obviously get it tucked in nicely on the rock. But sometimes it's easier to use the fish finder to find out where the nice big patch of rocks is to get your pots on top or down the side of the ledges.

If you're netting and the water's deep enough and you can drift over the top of the rocks, 'cause obviously sometimes you get a few bass hanging around over the top of the rocks but you don't wanna be hanging up on the rocks. It has been known to hang up, sometimes you get an anchor or something, I mean, sometimes you want to be in close for the bass, and then sometimes they're out to sea. Lot of times obviously where you're shooting North to South you'll only get fish on the inside end so obviously you want all your nets on the inside and then sometimes you'll get them on the outside end. So you try to get in as close as possible but with enough water so your nets are not dragging along the bottom but inevitably sometimes they'll hang up on an old anchor or something or other on the bottom and do a bit of damage but majority of the time you don't do a lot of damage, drifting.

Packing Up

I had to pack it in see, fishing because of money, simple thing really. It was just I needed something guaranteed every week even if it wasn't starting with the best wage and it wasn't as much as I was earning the majority of the time fishing. I mean I could have three months fishing earning a nice wage, every week but then I could have six weeks, seven weeks where you don't earn nothing. I mean it's alright if you've saved up for the couple of months when you're earning but when you're seventeen, eighteen it's not too easy to save the money you want; what you've got in your pocket you tend to spend at the time and really I needed something that was there every month, every week, guaranteed.

And with the Government making it harder and harder to fish all the time with all the regulations and the sea survival courses, you've got to do all the courses now, and the fish quotas and regulations on nets and the sizes of all fish you can catch, now they're talking about getting bass up to different sizes, and it's all just trying to stop you to go to sea and I'm convinced that its just making it harder and harder for you. And there's one of the lads, Michael Adams, over the beach at the moment and he's getting rid of his boat "Jamie" which has been decommissioned and he's just bought himself a little fibreglass fast working boat, it's all hauled up, ready to go, got all his nets and everything ready to go but he cant go to sea 'cause they've not been down. I'm sure it's the Coastguard that have got to come down and check it's all seaworthy and tick all the boxes, and well its just all paperwork and all the people in the offices justifying their wages and it is. But yeah they've been dragging their feet

I think he's been waiting two months, two and half months now and so he can't go to sea unfortunately because they're messing him around about getting his licence and all it is, is just transferring it from one boat to the other boat and obviously it's all money out of his pocket while he's not earning anything, but because they've not been down and done surveys on the boat, everything and the Coastguards not been along and he's not allowed to go to sea. I really don't know how it works. I mean, I thought it had of been simple job of someone coming down, looking at the boat, seeing it's sea worthy, ticking the box or doing something on the computer and saying "Yeah, it's all ready to go," but apparently its all different departments got a hand in it. If it had been me I think ' have been kicking up a bit more of a stink about it, but I mean, lucky enough, at the moment he's working third hand for one of the other fishermen, so he's able to earn money but if that was his only income, then I don't know what he'd do.

Life After Fishing

Ah, Id love to come back, yeah, Id love to if you start getting fish now like you was getting twenty year ago, thirty year ago, yeah, definitely. But, as I say, it's just the regular money. I miss fishing like hell, I really do. I mean, I'm fortunate enough now to be working the same hours. I mean, I'm up at crack of dawn every morning, I'm up half three, four o'clock most mornings and I'm finished by twelve, one, two o'clock at the latest most days. So that way it's not too bad. I mean I couldn't do a nine till five simply because of the hours I used to work as fishing. I'm used to getting up early, finishing early and to bed early sort of thing: with a few jars in between, obviously at lunch time!

Yeah, still love to go out, Dads boat's probably been to sea for its last time now; I regularly went out with him, any holidays I used to get off work, I used to be straight down here. Get a week off, get a weeks work with Dad, well, five or six days work with dad and really used to miss it after that. Used to have to go back, start driving around London again but get down here as much as I can, and as soon as Michaels' boats up and going hopefully we'll be going out, doing a bit of fishing on the wrecks and doing a bit of drifting for bass and that. Well, I mean obviously where I work I've got a regular job. I can't say to him "I'll be your crew" and go anytime but yeah, as soon as I get some time, weekends and after work if I can get away with going off for four or five hours after work, as long as it don't interfere with the job.

Difficulties In Fishing Nowadays

I don't think the money's in it nowadays. I mean, I sit here and say the money's not in it and then you see a couple of the new boats over the beach that are hundred thousand pound boats and you think, well if the money weren't in it how can they afford to buy boats like that. But, it's a lot harder and it's not going to get no easier. The government don't want any fishing. If they had it their way they would have the whole of this stretch along here, all along under the cliff, all the way along. They would have it as a nature reserve; a non-fishing zone, if they had their way that is. It's mainly the trawlers, I mean I'm not going to start pointing the fingers and everything but it's the trawlers that do the damage to the bottom. When they're using the heavy gear and they smash the bottom up and everything. The netters don't really do any damage, I mean obviously you get the occasional net you can't get back and they leave there and it will kill a few fish but I mean there's nothing that the eco system can't deal with, it's gonna regenerate itself. Our fishing down here is not a patch on anything. You could carry on fishing down here for hundreds of years, but when you see these big factory boats, I mean I don't blame 'em because they've got overheads, they've got bills to pay, but the French are a typical example of it. You go over to Calais or Boulogne and go on to any of the fish markets over there, and you'll see fish over there so small that you wouldn't even think twice about keeping it over here, you'd chuck it straight back over the side: and some of the tiny fish over there, I mean that's half the reason. I mean I remember the old man telling me a story that well must be twenty five year ago, thirty year ago: Him and Brian were fishing up on the East Hards, they had a fleet of four inch nets that they'd have been fishing in the rocks or something. They needed get rid of it while they went along to bigger mesh nets, so they slung it out, just chucked it out of the boat, shot it over the side, put it out properly just to get rid of it while they went and worked the other nets. And they'd only been in the water a couple of hours and they come back and they pulled it back and it was absolutely jammed full with little tiny "tommycods" and no one caught these what they call tommies, little small cods, no one caught 'em then. All they used to do was catch the big cods in the seven, eight, nine, ten inch mesh and so you'd obviously only catch the big cods so the system was regenerating itself. All the babies was growing up till they was big and you was only catching the big ones. 'Course the old man and Brian stumbled across all these little tommycods that you would catch in four inch nets so they thought well, "We won't say anything about it, we won't start going ashore and saying yeah, look, look, look!" 'cause obviously if you're catching all the little ones then none of them are gonna get big. So they didn't say anything about it. Obviously they got asked where they got the fish from and they just said they got them out of the nets in close and then for five, six, seven years nothing was said about it. No one fished for 'em, dad never fished for 'em, so obviously the regeneration was still going on and then people started catching on that you could actually fish for the little tommy cods and, as a result, I'm not saying that's the direct result of it, but obviously if you're catching all the little small fish they're not going to get the chance to get bigger and to regenerate the cod population.

I mean we don't affect the environment at all down here. We're but a blip on it compared to some of the boats you see. Some of the big factory boats, they're sucking up fish like you wouldn't believe, you're talking hundreds of tons of fish, where probably two of their hauls is probably all we catch down here in a month but I mean that's the way it goes. Someone's got a boat that's ten foot, the next man will have a boat that's fifteen foot, and then the next man will have a boat that's thirty foot and, and the bigger the boat the bigger the nets the more you're catching and obviously the bigger the boat the more money costs you got, so the more you got to catch and I mean, the running costs for these boats down here for these boats are absolutely nothing. Especially the netters, you get the diesel cheap and the engines don't burn any diesel really. If you're netting, you're just obviously just going to and fro the nets and steaming around a bit but you've not really got any overheads. You got maintenance of the engines and stuff but, it's the bigger boats that need to catch the fish to pay all the overheads.

There's not so many youngsters from the old families as there used to be. I mean there's a few, not really with their own boats; I mean there's a couple of lads down here that are my age that have got their own boats, but there's not really a great deal, I mean, no there's no real young uns, no one that's like up and coming, I mean you got the Adams's which are doing obviously really well over there, they've got a couple of new boats and stuff, but there's no real young 'uns that are coming through that are buying new boats. I mean Michael, that's all he's ever done all his life and that's all he's ever going to do all his life, that's what he knows, that's what he's good at, I mean, don't get me wrong he's good at everything he does, when he pretty much puts his mind to it he can do whatever, but fishing's what he knows, so fishing is what he will do.

MICK BARROW

28th of July 1943

Family History

I was born in Somerset, during the war, mother was evacuated down there. I was born in '43 at Wellington, we lived in Ilminster. My father was a baker, and his father was a farmer. After the war we moved back up to Hastings, in about '48 I expect. I've always been interested in fishing although I'm not from a fishing family and I more or less decided to go to sea when I was five, six, seven years old, something like that and I've been to sea ever since, many, many years.

I've got a brother who's a local boat builder, he's five years younger than me and I've got a sister that's a school teacher, she's down in Newlyn as it happens, down in Cornwall, and she's ten years younger than me. I was the eldest son.

First marriage lasted about four or five years, the children from that marriage were Michelle and Michael. Michelle is forty three now, so it was a little while ago. My second son, John, from the marriage with Linda, has been at sea with me from Hastings for five or six years. Then he got the wanderlust like I did and he went down to Paignton working, down in Devon. We got on well together, but we had arguments because he didn't seem to want to spend too many hours on the water. I had to earn money to pay for the house and keep the family really, but he just had his-self to look after so he didn't want to. But now he's a HGV driver, up four o'clock every morning, up to London, made up with it. Well he's older now obviously.

Fishing History

I started going to sea with what they called the part timers at Bo Peep, though there's none or very few there now. But it was quite a big community at Bo Peep of part timers. They had regular jobs but used to go fishing in their spare time. Alan George, there was quite a few, Freddy Frewin, lot of them worked, for the railway and I think there was a policeman there, but the majority was railway workers. Weekends I used to go with them, I was always over the beach putting lines down on the sand and bait digging for different people, and that was the childhood, that's what I did. I mean, it's not like it is nowadays, you could go out in the morning, eight or nine years old and come back in the evening late afternoon without any problem at all there wasn't any problem with these funny people who picked boys up and that, and girls, it was good.

I went to West St. Leonard's school, infants and then juniors, they've been pulled down now that was along Bexhill Road, on the corner of Filsham Road & Bexhill Road, then we went up to Woodlands which was a boys school and a girls school then they finished building The Grove, on the way to Hollington top of Harley Shute Road, after two years then I was there till I was fifteen. I didn't run away to sea, but I was encouraged to leave, when I was fifteen I went to the training College at Lowestoft, the Nautical College and then I went on the deep sea trawlers at Lowestoft and I worked my way up and I finished up third hand, boatswain and I was there for five or six years I expect.

I was a bit of a tearaway at school, nothing by today's standards I was really tame but then I was a bit of a black sheep of the family I suppose. I was five or six years, seven years at Lowestoft, saw an advert in the Fishing News, someone wanted a crew down at Lulworth Cove in Dorset for lobster and crabbing, phoned him up, "Yeah come down straight away!" so packed all me sea gear and I went down to Lulworth for two summers, but it was only a seasonal job and in the winter I went back to Lowestoft for four or five months. Had two years down there which I really enjoyed, it was like a holiday compared with the deep sea trawlers. Decided it was time to settle down, got married, moved back up to Hastings and started fishing at Hastings.

I thought about joining the Navy when I was thirteen and a half, you could join the Navy at thirteen and a half, training ship, Arethusa I think it was called, but decided there was too much discipline, so decided not to do that in the end, and that's why I waited till I was fifteen and went on the trawlers, there was just as much discipline but it's not carried out in quite the same way: you was told to do something and if the skipper tells you to do something, you do it. I mean, when you're at sea he's god, no doubt about it, you have to do exactly what he says. There's no one to complain to cause there is no one else there to complain to. Average crew on the Lowestoft boats was about ten or twelve, they wasn't real big ships, the biggest was about hundred and thirty foot, which is big compared with Hastings. We did two week trips, well, twelve day trips usually, two days ashore, that made your two weeks then you was back to sea again for another twelve days. That was on the big plaice boats: on the smaller boats, the boats that used to fish rough, for cod and haddock, the trips weren't quite so long usually, eight, ten days, something like that. They were smaller boats and it was hard work. With plaice it was a bit monotonous because you hauled every three hours, and it really did get monotonous. But on the boats that used to fish rough it was hard work, you was either mending or gutting.

By fishing rough I mean rough ground, with big bobbins on, instead of having a ground rope, small ground rope, you had big bobbins. Thirty six inch, then twelve inch and thirty six inch, to keep the trawl off the bottom, it used to roll over the ground. I mean the warps would be banging and cracking all the time, it was like fishing over the rocks and a lot of the time you used to tear the nets, and mend them up, or lace them up and you worked two sides at Lowestoft. If you smashed one side up bad you could unshackle the warps and shoot the trawl on the other side of the boat. And whilst you was trawling with that you could mend the trawl that you smashed up. Then, in between times you had to gut all the fish and all. It was shorter trips but we worked hard for the time you was at sea.

When I was down at Lulworth we was mainly potting for crabs and lobsters. The boat we worked there was about twenty eight, thirty foot, something like that, and she was anchored off in Lulworth Cove on moorings, too big to get up the beach in Lulworth. It was for the Miller family, Jim Miller I fished with, he's passed away now. Good as gold on the beach, in the pub, best bloke going: on the water he was a right misery, moaning and groaning. I didn't mind, I was quite used to being moaned at and listening to moans and groans from the skippers and that and I could take it. But I was the only crew that went back two years running with him, they couldn't handle him but I was alright, I didn't used to say anything, let him carry on moaning.

There was just two of us, and we used to go to sea daylight, and finish lunchtime 'cause I lived in with the family, had me own room and that. Always ashore by half past twelve, I think, was dinner, and that was it, dinner time was half past twelve and we was ashore by then, and in the afternoons I used to help one of the other brothers out, hiring rowboats out in the Cove, to make a bit of extra money, which was quite good, used to meet all the female holiday makers. I wasn't married then, better put that bit in! It was like a holiday really. I had two years down there and I never spent one night indoors.

I had my 21st birthday down there; that was the first year down there, then I went back the next year, then I met a girl, she was a holidaymaker down there, got herself a job and at the end of the season we both came to Hastings and got married, had a couple of kids, but the marriage didn't work out. Don't get me wrong, me and Margaret, my first wife, had some good times but it just didn't work, and I met Linda my present wife. Getting a divorce in those days wasn't quite so easy but got divorced, got married to Linda, another two kids and everything's all hunky dory.

I used to go bait digging, lug worm digging, quite profitable, and I used to dig for a tackle shop regular, well known tackle shop, not open now. And one of the clients was a bloke, Alan Richardson, who had a boat here and he said "Well he wants a crew, why don't you go and see him". So I saw his missus, they had the Mitre, antique shop up the High Street, and that's how I started at Hastings, in a punt. We used to go trawling, drifting and trammel netting, its when trammel netting really first took off: although there were trammel netters before I came down here obviously.

It would have been in '66 or '67, when the first daughter was born, and we just went from strength to strength, and I mean I had to learn all the grounds and bits and pieces as I didn't know anything about up this way at all, and I used to fish up Bexhill a lot which I knew the ground more up there, 'cause we used to live near the Bull Inn, when I was at school, and you learn as you get older.

When I was first married we had a flat along Marina, and I used to come along on a push bike along the sea front to go to sea. Then we had a flat in East Hill House, the garden flat, up Tackleway. But that was just for the winter, 'cause it was a summer letting place. Then we got a flat opposite the Stag in All Saints Street. Then we split up. When I married Linda we had a flat opposite the Fishermen's Club through the cottage improvement, Smith, the Estate Agent used to look after it. We had a flat there whilst they was doing another flat opposite the Piece of Cheese in All Saints Street, a maisonette, they did all that up for us and we was there a long while; we had both kids there. Then we decided to have a look round to see if we could buy a place somewhere but couldn't afford a place in the Old Town, because the Londoners were starting to come down then and buy everywhere up. So we got a place on the side of the East Hill in Boyne Road, it's cheap to modern day standards but it was a lot of money in them days and we've been there ever since, we're still there now. I like it, it's really nice and quiet, nice neighbours, and there's a playground at the end of for the kids, well, granddaughter now, we look after her half a week whilst her mother, my daughter, goes to work, and it's really good.

When I started with Alan Richardson sometimes we used to go trawling, night trawling and I learnt where all the ledges were at Bexhill and I could trawl in between them. Really lucrative because no one else had been there and I used to catch as much in the afternoon at Bexhill and then steam up to Langley for the dark and I used to catch as much daylight in Bexhill as I did dark at Langley.

Langley's just this side of Eastbourne, just East of Eastbourne. The punts don't go, well there's not many punts left now, I mean, when I first started I expect half the boats were punts, open boats and half were big boats that just went trawling. But the punts used to go trammel netting and trawling in the summer, and herring catching, they was versatile really, well you had to be, and it's the same nowadays really. You had your slack times but nowadays you've got all the Government restrictions and all the old rubbish that they can chuck at you.

In the sixties there wasn't any restriction on the catches, there was still the mesh size, but you weren't restricted on what you caught; you could catch anything you like as much as you like, as much as you could and I had a family to keep, a house to buy, wife didn't go to work. We agreed that she wouldn't go to work all the time the kids were at school, but if I couldn't make enough then obviously she would have to go to work. Anyway as it happens she didn't go to work until the kids left school, and you put money by for a rainy day. A lot of fishermen earned quite a lot of money one week and then go on the beer then go back to sea again when the money's run out. But I was never quite like that, don't get me wrong I used to have a drink! Fishermen, they've got a reputation for it! Even on the big trawlers, although you couldn't do it quite the same on the big trawlers, but you'd have two days ashore, if you was lucky you got three nights. If you got in after lunchtime you had three nights ashore, but if you got ashore before lunchtime you only had two nights ashore. On the big trawlers it was good money but it was hard work, and you could earn a good mans wage when you were sixteen years old. And it was recognised that you went and had a few drinks. Some people used to drink too much, but you always had to turn up to go to sea on the day that you was going to sea because if you got a bad name you didn't get a very good ship, you was on all the old rubbish which didn't earn anything You could always tell a decent fisherman by what boat he was on; if he was on one of the top boats he was a good hand, if he was on one of the crappy old boats, he wasn't a lot of good.

I fished with Alan about two years I expect. He was an antique dealer with his missus who used to look after the shop, and he was a dealer and he used to do valuations and everything. In the end he got a bit fed up with fishing and I said that I'd take the boat and he could stay ashore out the way. So that's what we did; I used to go on me own trawling, then when we was netting or herring catching I got a crew, and we used to work the shares accordingly: usually the shares in a punt was either three and a quarter or three and three quarters, it was a share for the skipper, a share for the crew, a share for the boat and a quarter share for the boy ashore who used to heave you up, see your fish on the market; and some of them used to make half a share for the gear. So that was the shares, on most of the boats. The big boats used to make four and a quarter shares but they was only trawling. The owner used to buy the gear for the boat; the skipper would say "I want so and so and so and so" and the owner used to get it, or the skipper used to go and get it himself and charge it to the boat. I used to look after the gear better then than I do now, now I pay for it myself, conscientious I suppose.

Well we had another boat built, a bigger punt and I said "Well look, I'd like to have half shares in it". So I bought half of the boat off of him, all pukka, all written down and that, so I was half owner of the boat. That must have been, round about 1976 I expect.

It was a clinker built boat with elliptic stern built by Phillips of Rye, and it was the first one that Derek Phillips built on his own. Then you had his father Harry and I don't think, it's building boats now, Phillips at all. In fact Derek's son is, or was the coxswain of the lifeboat at Hastings. I don't think you'll see any more wooden boats built at all, I honestly don't for one thing it's time building it, and another thing the wood is a lot more expensive now.

When we had this boat built, this last one, it cost, £2000, and £500 for the engine, and it was a fishing boat engine so they knocked £50 off. So that's £450 for the engine and £2000 for the boat: well it was a commercial enterprise. If it had been a yacht or cruiser or something then they wouldn't have knocked anything off. It's a negotiation really you know, you chat to them and say "Well we can go somewhere else or whatever." The boat is still here and I'm still using it; Conqueror II, RX55.

Well I half owned it and, I don't know what year it was, but I got fed up; I thought, well, Alan doesn't do anything, why should I give him half the boats' money. At that time he had got remarried as it happens to Peggy, and we was talking about my buying the other half. But I had it written in to the agreement when I bought half of it, that whoever sold out, sold at a reasonable price. So anyway, we had a chat, and it's when we bought the house, he said, "Well if you want the other half the boat you can have it." Well, Peggy, his new missus, she was interested in money, and the crew that was with me, Brian Skinner smashing bloke, really hard worker, reliable, he works over Eastbourne now for a fish salesman, he was interested in buying the half share rather than me. Well I thought, "I'm the skipper, so I make

Mick Barrow and Brian Skinner with RX55 'Conqueror II'.

all the decisions, so really it's putting money in his pocket and not in mine." And the reason that Alan said about selling the other half to him was because his missus knew that we'd just bought the house and put all the spare cash we had into the house to bring the mortgage down so 'course we didn't have a lot of money then so I couldn't buy it outright, I didn't have the money. And I think that's why she said to him to flog it and they would get more money off of Brian than he would off me 'cause I had it written into the agreement that it's got to be a reasonable price, but I suppose they could have asked twice as much off Brian. Anyway, I went along to the bank that we used, Lloyds Bank at the bottom of London Road, not there now, we bank there always and I used to do all the boats money and take it along there or whatever, or give it to Alan and he used to take it along, and it was alright, boats share used to just put in the bank, and the gear share. So anyway I went along to see the old boy, lovely old feller, proper typical bank manager, plus fours, pipe; so I went along to see him and said, "Look, I want to borrow the other half of the boat. I want a loan for it and I aint got no money", "Ah, ah, that could be a problem." So, anyway, we had a chat and well, I can't say too much cause I don't want to incriminate myself, but in the end he said "Well, I've looked at your books" he said "and you don't seem to be earning that much, to be able to pay too much back. Alright instead of you having a loan, you can have it as an overdraft and all you've got to do is pay back same as you are doing now, instead of the boat share going into the bank, that can pay the overdraft off." So that was really, really good, they wouldn't do it nowadays, and if you don't go to sea, you don't have to pay it. So really I didn't miss anything, I was still getting a share for taking the boat, and the crew was getting a share for being crew and the boat share was going in the bank paying the overdraft off. Brian wasn't very happy but there you go. I mean he stayed with us for a while, he was a good bloke but then he went fish hawking, selling fish out of a van. He used to have quite a lot of our fish 'cause he knew that I looked after it. I don't see the point in taking all the trouble to catch fish and then not looking after it when you've got it. Anyway he went fish hawking after that and I got another crew and crews aren't easy to get nowadays. Well, I don't blame them, young kiddies don't want it. My boy, he's regular money, regular hours, and he gets Sunday off, and Saturday every other week, and its regular money. But over here now 'specially with the government who want to get rid of you for a start, they've had their orders from the Common Market, cut the fleets down, which they've done. They started with the distant water trawlers in Iceland; that was one big con, you was on a loser right from the start with Iceland, the cod wars, they sent two or three gunboats up there, frigates, as a show of defiance, but the Icelanders, there was a NATO base on Iceland, the cold war was still going on, Iceland is the gateway to Russia, had a big NATO base there and what said was well if you don't agree to our, our new limits, take your NATO base away. 'Course you was on a loser to start with and it went out to fifty mile, and all the fish in Iceland are inside fifty mile anyway and then it went out to two hundred mile, anyway that's another story, that's beside the point, but that was the start of the diminish of the the distant water trawling fleet. Then the government bought the big trawlers that fished Greenland and Norway, they decommissioned them, the government paid for them to be decommissioned and that. There was still a few after the Falklands war, the boats that went out there, the trawlers, because they could stand the weather, I mean they'd be at sea when even the frigates wouldn't be there. But trawlers was still at sea as support ships anyway but they bought most of the distant water fleet, decommissioned them, paid the big owners. Boston Hamlyns, Boyd, Nurtmar, bought them all out and that was it, that was the finish of the distant water. There was a few freezer trawlers now, but nothing. I mean the British boats used to fish out on the Grand Banks and everywhere, Newfoundland, the Boston deep sea fisheries who I used to work for. They had trawlers everywhere in the Northern Hemisphere, everywhere. Lots of subsidiary offices; I nearly went to Nova Scotia on one of their boats, but decided against it.

We used to sell our fish on the market, yeah, there was a Dutch auction, which is: our fish is put in the scales, so the hawkers, the buyers can see it, and the fish salesman would start off say at £5 a stune. This is years ago, £5 a stune, and then he'd go down, £5, £4.90, £4.80 and the first hawker to up him, to stop him, say "Up!" they took what they want, they could have the whole, or so much of it, and that's a Dutch auction. But nowadays the auction has finished and there's just the couple of buyers now, that buy the fish wholesale. I mean the fishermen have got a co-op between them, that buy the fish and they pay for the fish, whatever they get for it, they take a commission out. And then there's Duncan Grant, he's been buying years and years and years over here, he used to buy all the fish that was left over on the market, after the sales and a lot of the fish goes to Bolougne from here. It's sold here and then goes across to Bolougne and well wherever, Ostend some of it, I mean some of it goes locally but there's not the call for some fish now; herring, mackerel, got a job to sell them. I mean, years ago, all the punts used to go herring catching, from September to Christmas, more or less. It's the punts that took over the herring fishing here, the open boats.

The big boats used to catch the herrings all round the coast, different times of the year you have to be in different parts of the sea. And the Lowestoft voyage was the end of August until October time. Then they used to go fish South, to the Sanditti bank, then they used to go down off the other side of Calais, it's a bank where all the herrings used to shoal on.

The Hastings boats, drifters had an agreement that they could dry their nets at the North Deans at Lowestoft. There was a big net drying area, with telegraph pole type things, you could stretch your nets across to dry after tanning, we used to tan them every now and again and they had the right to tan their nets and use the North Deans.

To start with, we used to go up to Lowestoft, the big drifters; they used to work nets 360 meshes deep. Much, much too deep for down here, but we used to buy so many nets and cut them in half, long ways. So they would be one hundred and eighty meshes deep, lot shallower, 'cause it's not so deep here and the old nets, they used to sew them, and the girls used to mend them all up, used to always have girls 'cause their fingers are more supple. And you could go up and buy 'em from Lowestoft, but the proper inshore nets used to be 200 meshes deep, if you had some made. But it didn't make a lot of difference anyway, but usually the herrings were more down the bottom, so the deeper the net the more herrings you catch. Same as mackerel, they're usually down the bottom, but bass are usually up the top. When you see mackerel on the surface they're usually after whitebait, they push them up and then come up the top after them that's when you can see them on the water. But sometimes it's shoals of bass after the whitebait or after the mackerel, I mean sometimes the mackerel will push the white bait so close that they jump out on the beach, and you can go along with a bucket and pick a bucket full up just like that where they have jumped out of the water to get out of the way of the mackerel, but you can't sell mackerel now; if you get ten stone of mackerel, that's as much as you can sell, just one boat. And yet, years ago not with mackerel so much, but with herrings, everybody went herring catching, till the government brought a ban in, what year it was I don't know offhand, it was in December, 1st of December they banned all herring catching, and we was catching herrings for Norway, many as you could catch, pound a stone which was good money then. Hundred stone, hundred pound, which was a good nights' work then. You didn't always get a hundred stone, sometimes you didn't get any at all, anyway, they brought this ban on, and we all stuck to it for that year 'cause we were finished herring catching Christmas anyway. The next year, still the ban on, and there's your Frenchman catching 'em, same herrings, same area more or less, selling them openly on Bolougne market, no one did anything about it.

It's supposed to be universal or European anyway, so anyway, then we said well, if the Frenchmen are going to catch herring, so we agreed that instead of having twenty nets which was the average fleet, we only had ten. And the herrings were guaranteed five pound a stone. So we made quite a lot of money out of that. Anyway, a lot of people got jealous, maybe fishermen even, that didn't have herring nets, or didn't go herring catching, and the Ministry of Agriculture and Fish, it's DEFRA now but it was MAFF till they had a cock up with the foot and mouth, and the fishery officer, lovely old feller, he called us up to the office, said "Look Mick, I've had so many complaints about all the herrings being landed", he said "I've got to do something about it" he said "I'm going to come down the beach tomorrow morning, nine o'clock. I don't want to see not one net, not one herring scale", he said "and if I do, then I shall take proceedings against you". So of course, come down, told everybody, made sure the boats were all scrubbed out, the nets were out the way, came down nine o'clock. It was alright, yep, no problems, no ones herring catching. But then it really got quite serious and we said "Well look we're going to go herring catching, and we're going to advertise it, in the media, and television". Got in touch with his bosses at Whitehall, and come back down to us, he said "Go ahead and catch them but keep it quiet". And that was that. Then the next year, well, I think the ban was on actually for four years, something like that.

It was in the new boat, we never went herring catching in the old boat. That was built '74, so it's probably late seventies I expect. Anyway, when they brought the ban back off, all the canners and everything had turned over to mackerel, or gone out of business and we couldn't sell 'em after that, can't sell herrings now, it's all finished. Plenty of herrings, sea's full of herrings, so it's preserved the herrings but no one wants them now. Most healthy fish there is to eat, with all the oil and that, omega food, but no, can't sell 'em because there's bones in 'em for a start. I mean, there's bones in every fish but there's small bones in herring and when you cook 'em, grill 'em or fry 'em, whatever you do, I mean I don't fry fish, I always grill 'em, trying to be a bit healthy, but they do smell. Housewives don't like smells. I mean I quite often have fish for breakfast, and the missus goes mad. "You've had fish for breakfast again!!" but that's a lot of it, and say, all the canners and the smokers and that, had finished. Lot of them had turned over to mackerel, so that ruined the herring catching.

There's still a tiny market for them, but there's not many punts now anyway, and you go herring catching, you get, say you get ten stone, that's about as many, as many as you want. But all the boats years could get hundred stone and get rid of 'em, but now if you got hundred say, I don't know how many punts there are, five, six now, if I went herring catching, got hundred stone each you'd just end up slinging them away cause you wouldn't be able to sell 'em. It's a shame, but there you go and that's the government and the boffins and the university herberts that come out of university and know it all. That's how they manage it, same with the cods now, see?

Seas full of cods. can't catch it; they won't believe the sea's full of cods 'cause everything's sort of written down and on a computer and that. "No, no, no, no, there's not that many cods." There is! We know! We catch 'em and we sling 'em away, hundreds. That's your scientists and your boffins, they only know what you tell 'em, and if you tell 'em something, they turn it against you, they work the other way. Years ago, Gummer, I think was his name, the fisheries bloke, had a permanent grin on his face, only a little bloke. He came down to the market; this was, in the early nineties probably. We just started using open scale drift net, not drift nets, gill nets for cods, seven inch. After Christmas he came down and we didn't know we could catch cods like that until we worked these seven inch nets. Well, seven inch net doesn't catch a cod under ten pounds, all the cods are over ten pound and after Christmas the cods are big, before Christmas they are usually small although now they're quite big now and no one worked seven inch meshes.

Well, 'cause no one knew about it and then, one bloke tried it, I mean we used six inch meshes, in trammel nets for plaice, and we caught big plaice that we never knew were there, 'cause the smaller mesh wouldn't catch 'em. Anyway, we was all working these seven inch gill nets for cods and this Gummer, the minister of fisheries then, he came down, we watered and fed him up the High Beech Club, he looked on the market which was absolutely full of big cods, all over ten pound; wasn't one other fish of any description on the market, just cods. He went back to Whitehall, put a cod ban on. So what you supposed to catch? I mean, would a politician agree to work for nothing? Well obviously not, but they expect fishermen to nowadays. With this cod ban on, we can't catch cod until next year as we've run out of quota. But we haven't run out of quota, there was pressure from the big boats on the government, for more cod, and they gave our quota to the big boats; don't worry about the small boats. The big boats have got more clout than what we've got. So, we can't catch cod now until the new year and then we've obviously got the quota anyway, which will be next to nothing. The quota we had this year, the beginning of the year, was something stupid, like it would have been three or four cods a day. That's all you could land; you're not going to make a living with that. Top and bottom of it is, government don't care, want to get rid of fishermen and that's the cheapest way to do it, starve 'em out of it and that's why you're not getting young kiddies taking fishing up now. Well I mean, there are young 'uns over the beach but not like there used to be and then as men retire, I mean I'm 66 now, and there's a lot of us in our sixties they're just not being taken over

I still go out; I don't do so much now obviously; for one reason, the mortgage is paid, I get a pension, I've got another pension. The missus has retired, she gets her pension, and she gets a pension from the Ashdown House, the ministry where she used to work, as a computer programmer. So we're not that bad off. I enjoy going to sea, in fact I went to Belgium to show the Belgies how to drift for bass, this last week and I enjoy doing it and I like to help other people and all if I can, it gives you a feeling of satisfaction. And I get fed up with doing the same thing, even when I had to go to sea, I used to get fed up with doing the same thing day after day, and I used to mess around and do other things, which some paid off and some didn't. But the bass drifting we started that down here and sometimes you earn quite a lot of money and other times you wont earn anything, bass are funny things. Do your 'ead in! One day you'll catch a good lot and you're raring to go the next day or night and shoot and got a heart like a lion and when you haul there's nothing, they're gone! Just like that, bass, ever such a fast swimming fish bass are. If the foods not there, they go elsewhere. But you know, it's something different, we earnt quite a lot of money with bass.

We only used to catch bass in the summer, when the water's warm. But the water's a little bit warmer now, even in the winter, and we catch bass all the year round, as long as you don't get Easterly winds. If you get Easterly winds you don't catch 'em. Don't know where they go, don't matter where you go, you don't catch 'em, 'less they don't feed with an Easterly wind. And if you get a cold snap you won't see any bass at all but if the wind stays South West, a mild wind, we'll catch them all the year round. When I was at Lowestoft they didn't know what bass was up there, and yet now they're part of the catch. And they're right up to Northumberland now, the bass. That's why I went to Belgium; they're catching bass now that they never used to catch.

You catch plaice more or less all the year; the best time is in the autumn, when they are thick. Just before they get rowed up, they're thicker fish. But you do catch them all the year. In the spring in Rye bay between the wrecks and that you get a lot of plaice, but they're not so thick, but people don't seem to worry too much about that now for some reason but years ago you know it all depended on the thickness on how much they made and everything like that but now it doesn't seem to make a lot of difference with the price.

We catch soles all the year round now which we never used to, as long as the wind's

Sou' West, as long as it's a mild wind. And the sole, we used to get a sole voyage, 'cause you used to get cold winters, snow and ice and lord knows what. And, the sole, what they called the sole voyage used to start, the end of March, usually and you used to get a lot of soles and the colder the winter, the more soles you got after it. Don't ask me why, 'cause I don't know, just one of them things. But they spread out all over the year now and we get spider crabs now that we didn't get years and years ago, we never got spider crabs. 'Course they ruin the nets they do, so you have to try and keep clear of them. I mean one lot of spider crabs and the fleet of nets are ruined. So we have to be careful, just work old nets or whatever. But you get soles all the year, but you used to before, you used to get them all the summer, but you used to get them trawling, you didn't get many in the nets for some reason, but in the sole voyage you did get a lot of soles, and I mean a lot. But now they seem to have evened out and you catch them all the time.

After John, my son, finished fishing, well when he left, I had two or three different crews, some of them weren't very reliable, used to earn, have a good weeks work one week, and you wouldn't see 'em; be on the beer. I prefer to go on me own now; Richard Reed is my boy ashore. He's only just over the road yeah, so I just ring him up when I'm going to go and say I'm you know, going to be half hour and he's already there for us. Yeah, he looks after me and another boat, a big boat that goes a lot more regular than I do. I mean he's older than me, I think Richard is, so we're all oldies really, we're all getting older together. They're mostly older now, well they always have been, boy ashore's have always been retired fishermen but there's not many young kiddies now. You've got the Adams family, they're young, and they'll be fishing, but how long it's going to last I dunno. It's a shame, and well, I can see fishing going downhill. Over the last twenty years it's halved in Hastings I expect, the boats and yet it's quite an attraction, I mean nearly all the holiday makers that come to Hastings, always come along the Old Town for the fishing and see the fishermen working. There's not many environments now you can actually see a working industry; most of 'em now it's all boarded up and this and that, and regulations and everything. But they're bringing so much in that you're so restricted now. It's not you know, as I said I've been to Belgium and they got just the same trouble over there. Just that the Frenchmen agree to everything, and don't bother to adhere by it and their government turn a blind eye but ours seem to work against you rather than work for you, so it's a bit disheartening.

Mick Barrow, wearing the Merit Medal for the rescue of fishing boat 'Simon Peter', meets the Queen Mother.

Lifeboat

I still enjoy fishing, if I didn't enjoy it I wouldn't do it it's as simple as that. I was in the Lifeboat for thirty odd years. You get all the comradeship and everything in the Lifeboat, but now there are no fishermen at all in the lifeboat. When I first went in the lifeboat, in the old wooden boat, 'Fairlight' there was six or seven crew, that was all there was. Everybody used to live in the Old Town; you didn't have pagers, you didn't have phones, just the maroons. And you'd get the two maroons; you'd always wake up of a night with the first maroon, time the second maroon went off you was out of bed and half dressed, and then you was down here within three or four minutes and if one of the crew, I mean quite often you used to be at sea, but then if you was at sea then it was reasonably calm anyway. And the coxswain used to say to the helpers, that's how you got in the lifeboat, you used to help launch it and recover it, and the coxswain would say to one of the helpers, "Come on, get a pair of boots on, you can come up with us". And that's how you joined the crew in them days. But now, I dunno, you fill a few forms in and you're one of the crew. I mean there's loads of crew. But then we could always find a crew, any of the fishermen would if the lifeboat was short handed any of the fishermen would jump in. But now they're not encouraged to, anyway I don't think. But, I dunno, I think it's a bit political all this with the lifeboat. Its got, well, Health and Safety and do gooders even crept into that now. With people suing and things and they've got to be so careful. I mean, lifejackets for a start: we used to have the old Kapok life jackets, uncomfortable, get in the way, so, when it was calm you never used to wear them. What do you want a life jacket for? But, if it was blowing hard, you didn't have to be told to put a life jacket on, you put one on, 'cause you know you might need it, but nowadays, if it's flat calm, you got to put a life jacket on, hard hats an' all now. We've got them (lifejackets) in the boats, we have to carry 'em. I don't wear 'em but it's always handy, it's there, which is, well, makes sense really, and you carry life rings and everything like that, well, board of trade, you have to so they're there, but you don't wear 'em 'cause they you can't work in 'em really. Or it's harder to work and they'd probably cause more accidents just by wearing one 'cause you're more restricted and everything with your arms and so they'd get in the way. I mean, don't get me wrong, they're a good thing, and they're there if you're going to be in trouble, put one on, or if you think there could be trouble, put one on. They're aboard the boat, they're all ready to put on, like fishing but we have to abide by regulations even with the fishing boat.

Five or six years ago, I had to go on two or three courses, sea safety... I've been going to sea fifty odd years, and they're telling you how to be safe at sea! Young kiddie, just out of university, knows everything, oh yeah, it's all written down in a book, yeah, it's in the book here! I've survived fifty years, you learn by your mistakes. The thing is you can't teach someone common sense, you've got to learn it yourself. Some learn it, some don't; some make the same mistakes every time, but others, you learn it and you make a mistake and think "Cor dear, I wont do that again". And it just comes natural, same as anything really, I mean a lot of problems are caused by panic, and people not stopping and thinking, not with fishermen but usually with yachts and things like that, they don't think. Oh quick, lifeboat, whereas if they was to think, they could probably get out of trouble themselves. Many times I've been in trouble then thought and got out of it; like, if you lose a rudder or something like that, that's all right, you lose a rudder, just put something over the side and pull it one way or the other. But you know a lot of yachts would call the lifeboat for that which, I mean they've not got the experience, but it's just common sense really. Anyway that's about as much as the lifeboat goes and fishing and that but I've enjoyed it, I've really enjoyed life.

STEVE BARROW

16ᵗʰ of December 1948

Family History and Early Years

I was born in Hastings in 1948, 16th December, well St. Leonards, in my Grans' front room in actual fact, that's where I was born. Always been in boat building, boat repairs; done an apprenticeship when I left school boat building, and I started on my own down here in August 1971, but before that, previous to that I used to work on the fishing boats connected with my job at Rye and also weekends used to come down here and do small jobs, so I've been down here probably since '65.

I left school when I was fifteen, whatever year that would be, first of all a job come up just building marine ply speedboats, and I've always liked fishing and messing about with wood, and I thought "Ah I'll try that, and then, knew it was okay but went over to Rye and done my apprenticeship at H. J. Phillips at Rye. They've just packed up now, well about a year ago they packed up, been there for three generations I think. It's a shame they packed up, yeah, but I suppose that's the way modern progress is. 'Cause Derek's son didn't want to take it over, he was happy with his lifeboat job and that's why Derek Phillips sold it. I think it's just for yachts now; they don't really build any traditional fishing boats at all.

My apprenticeship was five years, what they were then, now people go to college, I think they learn it in two years, I don't think you could beat hands on. Then it was all wooden boats. Just when I was about to leave it we started fitting out one or two fibre glass hulls, but majority were the traditional clinker boats, used to go all over the place, well all over the South Coast, far as Deal, Ramsgate, Brighton, all the way along the South East coast a lot for Dungeness, and for Hastings of course. There was a mixture then of all types of fishing boat, but all traditional clinker built.

Well there were one or two just a little bit over ten metres, because then there weren't restrictions on the fishing boats like there is now. Ten metres, yeah I think bout thirty three foot was the biggest one, and there were one or two clinker built cabin cruisers what we done. I think they were about thirty five foot or something like that.

My older brother Mick went fishing. I was thinking about it when I was at school I was thinking about what to do, but as I say this job come up doing these marine ply speed boats, and I've always messed about fishing, we used to mess about a lot at Glyne Gap in two or three row boats or outboard boats there and always used to be messing about over there and I used to like carpentry and that and when this job come up, I thought well they go together a bit so Ill try that.

The first job I had, the speedboat job, it was out the back of Marine Court, called Harold Mews it was, workshop in Harold Mews and then used to build for, well it's called East Sussex Marine now but then it used to be called Danny's Boy and he used to display them, and he used to be quite into selling speedboats and runabouts and, that's what the outlet was. They were all wooden framed and marine ply skinned, but they were all wood as well. I was there about two years, just under two years that was. Then I did five years at Phillips and left in '71, and then started down here on my own; yeah I was lucky in a way. I was doing a job for Tommy Adams, person who was unfortunately killed at sea and he let me have his net shop, well the bottom of his net shop, he said "You can start off with this" he said "you can do what you want in this." I had a little bench and that's where I started, and I bought the other net shops and the workshop next door and just progressed from there. In fact I'm back in there again now where I first started. I left it for a while, now I rented off another person, and I use that for a store really, but all in that area.

Boat Building And Repairs

I do mostly repairs. I have built well what you'd call row boats where you put an outboard on the back. I've done about half a dozen of them, where I am in the workshop there now, but mainly its repair, in fact the wooden boats getting less and less and have to diversify to glass and do quite a lot of metal work or steel work on the boats now. I've had to learn new things, I did go to College and do a welding course, but other than that, yeah, just self taught really with fibre glass, and a lot of the metal work. Mind at Rye when I done my apprenticeship we used to do quite a lot of metal work there, but not welding or anything and that is just progressed from the wood really.

Get on well with the fishermen, majority of them, get on well with them. Think it's a matter of having to 'cause they know that any problems they have to come along and see me.

I do just about all the Hastings work. Over the years there's been people come and go and think they're going to earn a fortune, but they don't last very long, so, yeah I do the majority of them. Not so much now, but in the past I have had to do general carpentry work in houses and flats just to fill in when I haven't got so much work on the boats. I will do anything with wood, windows, doors, floors, roofs, anything really. I don't work for other builders; just for people what might want a unit fitted, or might want a new front door or windows repaired, new flooring; just general things like that really.

Been working on boats for about forty years now, I've quite enjoyed doing it; I must admit in the days of the older fishing boats, when you were just looking for leaks, crawling about in the dirty bilges, that wasn't quite so good. Just doing a few copper rivets here and there, but every job has its bad side, but the majority of it is good. Doing a bigger job is nice where you can get stuck into planking and ribs and frames is good. Usually comes about probably due to wear and tear or sometimes damage. Sometimes damage 'em, not so much with the new boats, but on the older boats if they go off in any sea sometimes they're holed when they swing round get knocked round in the surf and rolled about on their bilges and knock a big hole, probably about half a dozen boats that has happened where there's been a big hole, some of them you could walk through the side where they knocked so much timber out. As I say, not on the steel boats but on the wooden boats, when they're knocked round underneath the banks when they get pounded by the sea they do quite a lot of damage. Sometimes have to re-build from the bilge keel upwards.

Clinker built is the traditional way of building; I think it originated from the Vikings. In fact if you go up to the Maritime Museum, you can see they're so similar, boats what they've dug out the mud what have been there for hundreds of years and you can see where the boats at Hastings have got the idea of general design, type of building. It was so similar, clinker is overlapped normally about, depends on the size of the boat but anything from an inch, to about three quarters of an inch and that's called the land, the bit that is overlapped, and that's riveted together and that's all what stops the water, just the tightness of the rivets, stops the water coming in. Traditionally the timber is elm, Wych elm which is very durable, bends well, and for the sea I think its very good timber. Elm in fresh water isn't so good 'cause it rots quite quick but in the sea water there's nothing better. When they had the Dutch elm disease and hurricane it was a job to get elm in. A lot of people changed over to mahogany but to me it doesn't seem to be so good as what elm does.

Wych elm is a type of elm; there's a lot of different species of Elm, and that is just one type of elm. Dutch elm is another one; although it don't come from Holland it's called Dutch elm. Now it's very scarce, it's a job to get elm now. I think there's still some growing in Devon and still some up in Scotland. The last lot I got come down from Scotland; not by me, but that was through a third person and that come down from Scotland.

The planks are cut and overlaid and fastened with square copper boat nails which go through, and you put a rove, that's punched on the inside and with somebody holding a maul, (a type of big hammer,) waits on the outside, rivet over. The more you rivet it the tighter it gets, each one done individually by hand; depending on what boat it is, about every two and a quarter inches; a square copper boat nail its proper name. It's predrilled and it's knocked in with a dolly on the inside, to stop it bouncing, knocked through, then when its held on the outside with a maul or dolly to stop the nail and going back with a hollow punch, the rove is punched on, like a washer, like a round copper washer, its punched on, snipped off and riveted over. When you're nailing it through, you put all the nails in that plank first, and then somebody on the outside would hold on the head of that nail and the person on the inside would punch the rove on, snip it off about, an eighth of an inch past the end of the washer and then rivet it over with a ball pein or cross pein hammer. That is traditional. I think on the Viking boats they would have just used steel. It looks very like they would have used steel fastenings and on some French boats what I've seen they only use steel fastenings. Obviously the copper, well, the copper would be more durable I should imagine. Now, caulking, the only place you caulk a clinker boat is down the stem, along the keel, and up the stern post. That's the only place you caulk a clinker boat as opposed to a carvel boat where the planks are flush, and you caulk every seam, every joint between the plank they're all caulked,

Steve Barrow meets the Queen Mother.

but on a clinker boat, its caulked just along the keel and up the stem where the planks end on the stem. So the rest of it just depends on the rivets and holding the boards together and swell up the tightness of them, swells up on to the rivets on contact with the water. Well, the first time any clinker boat is put in the water they do normally leak, or if they're laying up in the summer, when they have their paint up and that, when they go back in the water they will leak for the first two or three trips, some quite badly.

'The Valiant', was probably the biggest repair job, I'm not sure about the year, '72,

'73 maybe, that was in a collision with a coaster, and I think there was about six or seven planks all smashed in and quite a number of ribs, and there was quite a really big hole in that. They were lucky to get it back ashore in actual fact, most of the damage was just on the water line an' above it what they done at the time of the collision. I was out there in the inshore lifeboat at the time. We moved all the ballast and everything over to the other side, that wasn't damaged, to try and get the hole out the water where it was damaged, and she was towed in stern first so she was away from the sea, so the sea didn't wash into the hole, and yeah it got her ashore. It was about five miles off of Fairlight it was. In collision with, I think it might have been the "Frederick Hughes" the coaster. Unfortunately somebody lost their life on it, George Mitchell, "Gammy" was his nickname, but yeah, he was killed in the accident and the other person was well obviously shaken up and I think he had a broken arm.

Lifeboat

I first started off with the lifeboat when I first started working for myself down here in '71 and then sort of progressed on to the offshore boats and finished up as assistant mechanic, after twenty two years. I started with the inshore boat which had a crew of two or three. I did keep on with the inshore a lot of the time because I was so handy, working here on the beach, sort of always around. I used to do both in actual fact. There was about eight or nine crew on the offshore boats and obviously a couple of reserves, and on the inshore boat I think there was about six or seven, not all at the same time. Summoned by a maroon and phone then, now they have pagers and bleepers but then it was by phone and maroon and the inshore boat it was a klaxon, they don't use the maroons now, the crew have pagers and so they don't use them or the klaxon now I don't think either.

Had to go out for all sorts of things; the inshore boats was quite busy in the summer with a lot of swimmers, wind surfers, smaller boats what had broken down, rowing boats that couldn't row back. The offshore boats obviously that was normally a different type of rescue, right from ships where you had to go and stand by, people washed overboard from ships. Collisions, yachts and fishing boats breaking down, leaking badly. At that time it was all fishermen on the offshore boat, the inshore boat wasn't so many fishermen, they did have different people from different walks of life but on the offshore boat it was all fishermen at that time and it kept to all fishermen, or people connected with the beach, there was a boy ashore, but the majority was fishermen. Now unfortunately, I don't, there's no fishermen at all on it which, in my personal view, I don't think it's so good because professional seamen is much better than somebody who sits in an office all day. I think it's got more regimented now, and I think it's got more regimented and perhaps the fishermen where they had to send you on courses to do everything in whereas commercial fisherman knows. They send you on courses how to tie knots and seamanship and when I was there everybody knew that anyway.

I mean, Health and Safety, the lad who works with me, a really nice lad, he's just joined it and he's got a Health and Safety book they give him, and it's full of just common sense rules; how to climb a ladder, how to put a ladder up, and it's just common sense really.

Changes

Fishing is changing but I think the fishermen are still the same in actual fact. Perhaps being down here every day you don't notice the change, but I think they're still the same. It's not the younger people coming into it now as what there used to be. When I first started there was a white fish authority then, that's a branch of the government what run it and they were giving grants to have boats being built, now it's the other way round, they're giving grants to have the boats, taken out of commission and demolished really. And there was also a grant, or subsidy on fishing, on plaice, which they give you, I forget what, about half a crown a stone, something like that and now they're stopping you catching fish so that side has changed so much. I think more now the youngsters want a regular wage, where fishing isn't regular at all. Just this last couple of weeks I think that one trip they might have had, maybe three weeks it's been blowing, one trip, two trips, and there's just not the regular wage there, the people want a regular wage now, all the fishermen what have got out of fishing, they said it's the best thing they've done you know, there have been fishermen that now work on the railway, postman, gone to the post office and they said, nice regular wage coming in, you know.

I do have the same problem in the winter when there's not a lot of work about, but it's swings and roundabouts isn't it. In the summer when it's nice weather you don't mind working, in fact, well I enjoy it all the year round, but it's really nice when it's nice weather and you're working outside on an interesting job, but in the winter when it's blowing hard and freezing cold and it's a bit different you think "Oh I should be inside in a nice warm place." The lad with me now, well I haven't really taken him on, he comes along, he's at college now, he comes from

Latvia, been over here a couple of years, and he's really keen. He wants to do yacht designing or yacht, ship designing when he leaves college, very keen lad. Well, in fact he's shipped two boats over here from Latvia. They've been transported over here, two more boats what he's doing up and he's done well. They are just outside me workshop, one little one, just a rowing skiff, clinker built one, the same which he's put all the planks in and he's doing the ribs now, and he's making a good job of it. One of them's carvel built, but the little skiff he's doing, that's clinker built just the same way as the Hastings boats to be honest. His little boat was built of pine obviously in Latvia there's a load of Pine forest and probably in Scandinavian countries they would have built them in pine. As the Viking ships were I believe, there's so many pine trees over there.

Hastings Boats

We don't have carvel boats at Hastings, with a carvel boat they move too much on the beach, and where they caulked the seams, that's the joint between the plank, they would tend to move more, and all the caulking would come out and they would tend to leak more. Carvel boats are more for harbours. You do get a few on the beach, but not on Hastings beach, I don't think there's ever, fact I don't think I've ever seen any on a commercial fishing beach. Difference with Hastings boats, traditionally they would have been flattish bottom for the beach so they don't draw so much water, so they can get off the beach easier. The stern would have been an originally elliptic stern, or a lute stern, as opposed to a transom stern in a harbour; just a flat transom stern in a harbour. Whereas a lute or elliptic was to keep the sea breaking inboard the boat and also to give it more lift as you're getting off the beach. They are changing now and a lot of the steel boats what are on the beach here at Hastings they're built with a flat transom now. One of the reasons is because now they all have the tractors and bulldozers to push them afloat they can get them afloat much easier; whereas originally it was just manpower that got them afloat, there was no tractors or bulldozers, and you needed a boat what would easily lift in the sea, as opposed just to pushing into the sea with a bulldozer.

I still get enough work with other bits of general carpentry I do. Yes, 61 now and a few more years will be me, well I don't really want to retire, just do two or three days a week, and that will suit me. I don't know if I will pass it on, I doubt it, there won't be nobody. As I say the young lad who's with me now, he won't; in fact I wouldn't want him to stay down here because there wouldn't be the work for him down here. I've noticed it in my time, there's less and less boat work to do, and I do more general carpentry and I think he would be the same, there definitely wouldn't be enough boat work down here to keep him going because they're mostly steel and there's a lot less number of boats here now. I don't know what the number is, twenty five, twenty something like that, whereas when I first started I think there was about thirty five, forty boats down there and they were all wooden boats of course, so obviously I was kept really busy all the time just planking; putting in planks and doing planks.

You used to get rows over whose boat should be done first yeah, when they wanted to get back to sea and if I was doing something to somebody else's boat and they were laid up and couldn't go to sea, they just have to grin and bear it. I can only do one job at a time.

'Edward and Mary' being re-decked in Steve Barrow's yard.

GRAHAM COGLAN

17ᵗʰ of January 1938

Family History

I was born seventeenth of the first '38, in Scrivens Buildings, which used to be up Crown Lane. I can remember the war and I can remember coming down on to the beach and crawling under the barbed wire, big fences what they had up and getting into trouble many times through that. From then on I remember the bomb landing in High Street, it was in the Swan Pub in the High Street that some chappie run down the road, picked me up and threw me into the toilet of the one down the bottom of Crown Lane, forget the name of it.

With regards to many other things, just the normal, as a lad would do: schooling when I was an infant was up round the Croft, I can't remember the name of the school there: It's many years ago obviously, and that was when the war was still on. And then from there I went to All Saints infants school which was up All Saints Street, from there I moved on to the junior school of All Saints, and then from there, had quite a long time in hospital with rheumatic fever, then I was moved on to St Mary's in the Castle. I was lucky, 'cause I used to play football, and I played football quite a lot then.

After that I went in the army when I was eighteen. When I come out the army in '59 then I went into the building then, I was bricklaying 'cause I used to do bricklaying in the army: and we built up our own team then, and we employed about forty people at one time you know, getting on, we had such a lot of work to do, and we done very well. We was a very well known firm and for a few years I was doing very, very well bricklaying. My brother, Roy Coglan, he was about two years younger than me, worked with me, he died nine years ago, in 2000, and he started going fishing out of Rye, he was also a bricklayer at the time. He's probably one of the best bricklayers you've ever seen, but he finished and went fishing and I thought, well, if it's good enough for my brother, it's good enough for me.

Fishing History

He bought a boat and we went to Scotland to buy it. It was something like '73, '74 when we went up to Fraserburgh, Scotland to buy the "Daybreak". We'd never been that far before anywhere and we brought the boat down the East Coast on our own, got lost many times coming down, as you can imagine. But we made it in five days it took us to come down.

So, I bought a boat, only I bought a smaller boat, a punt, and we had it named 'Nichola Darren' after our children, the two children we had then. I had it built at Rye, it was only a small punt and from then on it was fishing, fishing, fishing all the time. The other one I had come from along the West end, NN51. I bought it off of some anglers along there. Then I had the two boats working off the beach, both punts but after that, it increased. I had, the 203 which was the "Nichola Darren", 204 'Simon Lawrence'; we had that built at Rye, and 51 was the one we had from Newhaven, then we bought one called "The Mandy Ann" off of Jimmy Simmons who used to be the fishery chairman.

After that we had the Yellow Peril built by Charlie Todd. He was a boat builder as well as a builder: he built it in London. It wasn't the type of boat you had on the beach really. We managed it perfectly, really, really nice little open boat. We had a forward wheelhouse, and it was painted yellow all the time. We had it yellow, same as my boat now, all the time. Real name of the boat was 'Los Hermanos' 'cause as I say he was into Spain and all that, all the time. He suggested that, so where he built it for us we named it that: it was named that but we always called it the 'Yellow Peril.'

We done extremely well in the first years of fishing, 'cause fishing was good then and now we're coming to the latter part of it, where we are aging, and it's not so good fishing.

Harold Pepper owned 'The Enterprise' and my father was his crew for a long time and when Harold retired, he bought a house off me up in Bembrook Road, and we got on very well together but my dad was there for quite a long time and of course all of my family on my mother's side, were fishermen. The Peters family: Jack Peters was the oldest fisherman I know over here when I was a kid. He was 82, and he used to come with me in one of the "Yellow Peril". My uncle Jack come as a crew too, and he was 82 then and he done everything he needed to, he was a good hand. My father's dad wasn't a fisherman. We come from Bishop Auckland, Durham go back over the years they're an Irish family but he come down in the Jarrow March, 'course, met me mother and got married and that was it: go back a long way and it's Irish family.

I was fishing before I was 36 because we were what we call part timers; which we wasn't very well liked for by the fishermen out here. We had a boat along St. Leonards, fishing at the start. I was still building at the same time like: actually we built that big building along there at Bulverhythe. My brother fished the 'Daybreak', for three or four years I should think. I continued building for a while 'cause we had such a lot of work on and such a good income, so we stayed doing that.

I had quite a few crews as you go through life and that, and through the time we was fishing, we had a crew called Dicky Doughnut, I cant think of his second name now. Yeah, Dicky Doughnut, he's a big guy and he gets in the angling club quite a lot and he took the boat after I left that, went into a bigger boat 'cause I bought another big boat off this end. The one I bought off this end first, I believe was when Tommy 'Toller' Adams, lost his life in it. That was just out the end here, I bought that one off of Wilfie Adams: he had it first, and then I bought it off of him; I can't think of the name of it.

We were trawling mainly and trammel netting. In the punts it was trammel netting, when we got into the bigger boats it was all trawling, then in the bigger boats, and then I went to Dover, and bought the boat what Brian Stent had built. Brian Stent was a well known Hastings fisherman; very good fisherman, and he sold it because it fell over one day, and come over on to the other bilge, and he had his knee underneath it, and it smashed all his leg in. So he sold the boat 'cause he was out of work for a long time, on that. Somebody from Dover bought it and it laid in Ramsgate Harbour and I went over there with Joey White, and 'cause he had a couple of boats on the beach then, and we bought it over there for about £12,000

I think it was. Brought it back and that's the boat we've got there now: RX60 'St Richard'.

RX60 'St. Richard' now renamed 'Alfie Elliott' by Graham Coglan after his grandchildren.

Fishing in the Past

In the seventies, fishing was good. We were catching all types of fish. We was allowed to catch all types of fish. There was no quotas, no, nothing like that at all, so whatever you wanted to catch, you go ahead and try to catch it, if you caught it you could bring it ashore and sell it that's why we done so well then.

Its all seasonal, 'course in them days going back a lot of the years, herring catching was very good here, and then say from late September through till December you was herring catching, and they was when all the punts come in handy. One time there was about oh, fifteen to nineteen I would say, punts, anchored in the harbour, waiting to go away in the dark, to get a berth, and herring catching was very, very good then. You only catch the herrings in the dark; you don't catch 'em in the daylight, and then you was catching an enormous amount of herrings; and very bad job to sell 'em. Where you was catching such a quantity, and sometimes you could go off say three o'clock in the afternoon, steam down to under the cliffs, anywhere down there, wait till just twixt lights, put your nets out, lay there for about an hour, lift 'em up and have a look. Sometimes that's enough, you come ashore, unload 'em, and then go away again three or four o'clock in the morning, providing the tides work that way, you done a double whammy at it, and you done very well at it. So before twilight you put your nets out, pull 'em in if you've got a decent catch and then ship your nets again. Come in take all the fish out, put the fish on the market and then go straight off again. We laid there all night.

In winter is cod fishing. Doing very, very well at that, 'cause there's always been a load of cod in the Channel hasn't there? There is now, there's an abundance there at the moment, and there was then but we didn't have the amount of gear in them days, as what you've got now. You got more modern gear now, and it proves itself time and time again. You used the old trammel nets as opposed to these kit nets what they've got now. The kit nets are four or five times better because they're a different mesh, everything's different about them. These are made of nylon, and cat gut type, they totally different nets.

In spring we didn't do a great deal of mackereling but some of the punts, they had what we call a seine net, and they would shoot them in the harbour, or round the other side of the harbour, and they'd get quite a good quantity of mackerel there but there was never no great amount coming in from the boats going mackerel fishing. They did go out obviously, and they caught mackerel, but no great bulk of it.

In summer you'd be sole fishing and you got plaice, but you don't catch plaice in January to April that much, 'cause they're all very thin but anywhere after April and you can catch plaice as well, but they only go through 'til about November, then you don't see many of them.

Most of my fishing was done in Rye Bay and I went to Ramsgate quite a lot in the punts. We went out to Ramsgate in the winter; because when you get a south westerly wind up there you're covered you've still like a landy wind here, a northerly wind here. So you can get off each day, as we left the boat at Ramsgate anchored up in the harbour we used to leave here at six o'clock in the morning, go to Ramsgate in the car, go and have a good breakfast and go off in the boat, do the nets, and come back in again. I had a big boat up there as well "The Daybreak", the one we went to Scotland for. My brother bought another boat by then, and this chappie from Ramsgate, he took the boat for us, but that wasn't a success be quite honest. Cost us quite a lot of money on that; he wasn't a very successful fisherman I was getting a share from it but I think we paid out more than what we got there and we sold it to somebody from the Channel Islands, and we nearly come unstuck then because there was the government grant on it and you have to pay the grant off back to the government, and we didn't realise that, but anyhow, it wasn't too much.

The Crews and Boats

I'm still fishing now in the yellow boat it's got a different name now, 'Alfie Elliott', my grandson. We changed it from 'St Richard', that's what Brian Stent named it, 'St. Richard'; we changed it now to 'Alfie Elliott'. I go out with the oldest fisherman on the beach, David Peters, from the Peters family my cousin, Uncle Jack was his Uncle Jack and his dad was, a Peters of course. Sometimes I take my nephew, because he's had a lot of illnesses, cancer and whatever; he's coming back this week again and I've had a lot of crews, through the years mind, a lot of crews, and David's been with us now for a number of years. He's 72, coming up 73. His nickname is Spider, I always call him Spider, he is probably, the best fisherman working on the beach I would say; he never stops, he's always doing something, he's always busy, if he's not making nets he's making pots, making trows, he's always busy, always works bloody hard he does and he's so fit for his age, he's amazing. Unfortunately, my son, he's had terrible cancer, and he was only given two months to live, when he was in his twenties but now he's in his forties and he's still here, and he's working on the beach with us but he's still has to go up every six months to The Royal Marsden for, you know, check ups and that. And just recently last year, he's had to have another operation, they found a tumour in him again, and they had to take that tumour out. And so he, Lawrence, his name is, you'll probably see him on the beach along there, he goes mostly with my nephew, Darren, on RX 150, Roy's Boys he goes mainly with him, but my daughter, she doesn't work now, she was an air hostess for thirteen years, and lives up Old London Road, we all live in there together, all in there. We bought that between us: it's a big place and we built Lawrence a home in the garden, you know he's got a nice home in the garden, big shed we built for him. He's got everything in it, you know, all the mod cons and shower, toilet, and everything in it. And me daughter, and her husband and our grandson, live in the main one with us. We've built on the end to make it a granny annexe as you call it; we live separate like.

Good Times

Apart from hard work, memory makes a good fisherman: where you was, or writing it down where you was, where you caught the fish and, all things like this. I mean, go back twenty, thirty years, I used to go angling with the boat, and take the anglers off with me like, keep the fish what they caught, but it was all wreck fishing. You go to wrecks, different wrecks, and them days you didn't have 'Decca' or anything like that, you had a sounder, an echo sounder and a compass, then you go out, but you could only go out on the really good days so you take all the land marks, line two things up to go where you're going, and time yourself to get to that place. Then when you got to where you think it is, by your land marks, then your sounder, you would throw a dan, then work that dan, keep going round and round and round until you found the wreck, but we got so good at it, it didn't take no time to find them. Then I could find thirty one wrecks just by landmarks, which was extremely good, with the help of my crew of course, yeah it was extremely good, and we caught loads and loads of fish. We went, the angling festival one year, I can't remember the year the top nine prizes were on my boat for the amount of fish they caught, the biggest fish they caught, and yeah, top nine prizes, we done extremely well. They take home what they want but then what's left you put on the market, and it's all congers and cods them days, mainly. It was all for pleasure mainly when we went wreck fishing. We went out to what they call the 'riddens' that's about eleven twelve mile off the French coast, South East from here, and we had a storm fishing up there then, angling, the lads were, angling. About two hundred and sixty stone we caught there that one day, and brought it home. 'Course lads took home what they wanted, 'course there was hell of a lot left, and that was mine on the market; made a lot of money on it but we had bad days don't forget.

Bad Times

Fishing in Hastings has declined, you see the youngsters that are coming into it now, there isn't any. There's very, very few youngsters coming into it. You look at the people on the beach that go single handed now; it's just on their own. That's out of order that is, they should never, never go to sea on their own. I know it happened a long, long, long time ago when Tom 'Toller' lost his life through being on his own. Got caught in his winch didn't he, but the lads now, my brother, you got the sign down by the market there, he lost his crew; he went over the side in the net. They couldn't find him you know, pulled all the nets up, he wasn't in the nets at all, they washed out the nets and they never did find his body. I think its got to a point now, if we don't win this next meeting regarding quotas, if we don't get anything there, I think it's going to go downhill fast again, I really do, 'cause we're not allowed to catch cod: it's criminal throwing dead cod back. What happens to it? It makes me angry, it really does, 'cause as I say you can't think there's going to do any good to anybody really. All it does is rots on the bottom of the sea, dead cod, you get all five fingers on it, you know, and little whelks and all the winnets and that, all get on it eat all the flesh off it, then you get all rolled back into your net again, stinking, you have a job to get 'em out of your nets, you really do, 'cause of all the bones sticking out, and you have to pick out, bit by bit. No, it's terrible, and I mean, how can anybody think that by throwing them back its going to help the fishermen? It can't, its impossible. All it does to us is make more work for us, and less money. Live cod won't survive 'cause they've got an air bladder, and that air bladder's got to be pierced, so the air comes out 'fore they go over the side. You could do that if you had the time, you could take a syringe with you and prick it but who's got the time to do that if you're out in half a gale of wind, you're bouncing up and down like a yo-yo: try doing it then. You can't, its impossible and, well, you know as well as I do it's just stupid.

A Typical Catch

On a typical day I'll give you an example of a catch, last week we went out, different place. We'd been fishing up off Bexhill just under a mile off the shore, so I went out another half a mile, this side of the buoy, one fifty off the shore. You put three fleets of nets down. First fleet there was nothing in you know 22 soles, two or three cods: The next fleet, which was a different type of fleet, it was one of these ones

I was telling you about just now we hauled it in and there was cods coming out, just hand over fist, and I mean that, you know. We reckon there was between thirty and forty stone in that one fleet. Now if you got eight fleets down, what you gonna catch, three hundred stone? Ah, its ridiculous, so all you have to do is take them out and throw them back over the side and that takes longer to do it you know, 'cause you have to get the fish out the bloody nets before you can chuck over the side, then you've got to pull your nets over and pack 'em to go and shoot them somewhere else, but we had that I can honestly say now, sitting here, that that is the most fish I have ever caught in one fleet, cods that day throw 'em all back. That was about a fortnight ago. This particular quota that we're talking about is the way that the quota is divided up by our government. We have got no quota, all we got I think is about hundred and fifty ton between area 7d. Paul Joy will tell you more about that, he's got a very good retentive memory, he has, he can remember everything about it, I used to be able to, go back a few years but can't now. And, when you share that out between about 300 boats in 7d that area what you got to catch? Nothing, nothing! We got 44 or 45 ton for 7d, and that's for a year. You've got 300 boats in the area. I mean gone in January. So, you got the rest of the year for nothing. I talk about 7d. We're here now aren't we, go over the other side the French are there aren't they, they got, the French are included in 7d, got 76.4% of the cod quota, 76.4%!! We've got 8%. Just shows you, you got nothing. You know as well as I do Ted Heath helped the farmers, but destroyed the bloody fishermen, that's what he done in his day it's devastating, it really is devastating.

Still At Sea

I have enjoyed myself fishing. That's why I do it, that's why I still go to sea now I enjoy fishing, but going back through the years I can't actually remember when the worst one came in, but I can remember the minister coming down here on the market, when we had a cod ban before, and I got caught out here with the cod aboard but I told a lie and I told them I caught in 4c, that's round the corner into Hythe Bay, when what we was then off of, not quite that far down and I got away with it type of thing but I had cod on board when they boarded me. The warship like, you know the navy, it might not be navy, it might just be navy boats but fishery officers on it, and then because I said I was on 4c, they put the boat on the tip of Dungeness for two weeks. They anchored there for two weeks to make sure nobody could go down and come back with anything; catching down there we were allowed to fish in 4c. They wasn't stopping you, you could go down there, but you had to prove you was going down there, they could prove it that way. Ah it's got into a nasty, nasty way of being now.

All I can remember is good times you know, one time we took the fisheries from up North what are they called? Oh, blowed if I know, can't remember but we took them off fishing on the other side of the hole, that's about five mile out and they wanted, Paul's got it all on a video I think, to put five fleets of their nets down: so they put them five fleets of nets down, I put two fleets of my nets down, I had a seven inch mesh, they started from three and half inch mesh up to a five inch mesh, and then we went and had one haul down through the hole, we call it 'the hole', in the sand out there. One haul down through there, while I was waiting for the slack water, so we let them fish for two or three hours then picked the nets up. We put the trawl over the side, and they had scientists on board, with me like the old fish scientists, and we got the trawl up and we had so much plaice in it, it was untrue and we only had hour and a quarter with net down. We lifted it up and we had well over hundred stone of plaice, all big plaice, 'cause they had five inch mesh cod end, you know. They was made up with it, so was I, and then we went up and picked the nets up. We got these nets up and the small mesh nets had quite a lot of fish in. Whiting and stuff like that, but no good fish. Then they got to the end of theirs, we're five inch mesh and they had some nice plaice in, good plaice. Then we picked our two seven inch mesh up. Big plaice, all good fish, and they said when we went back we had a meeting in London, and they said this was the most economical and friendly way of fishing as can be devised. And that's what they put through on big screen, up in London; and that's why we've got a certificate of approval for fishing in Hastings 'cause of that type of fishing. What the bigger mesh does is it catches the bigger fish, but all the smaller fish can get through and breed and you don't catch the little tiny fish, so, they can grow up and breed, but if you go back down to the ninety mill what they're using now, that gets all the tiny fish, and they have not bred so therefore you're not going to get no more quantity are you? Four or five years ago we put in for an upgrade in the mesh to one hundred mill, it nearly went through, but then the French disagreed with it. So through Europe, got it stopped. But it nearly went through. We use hundred mill, we don't use ninety mill but a lot of boats on the beach do, unfortunately, and you catch little tiddlers. Soles you catch would be about nine inches unfortunately that's what's happening; 'cause they don't grow, they don't breed, they don't get a chance to. They've all go to be a special size. We've got the chart on board the boats which say what sizes each breed of fish has got to be; if it's too small it goes back. There's two or three breeds of fish what we're totally against, because turbot, brill, fish like that, quality fish you can catch 'em that big. There's no law against that. You don't have to worry at all about any sizes on them. There's several other fish as well, you don't have to worry about.

But the turbot and brill which are you're two prime fish, ridiculous. They don't get a chance to breed. This is your boffins, your scientists and your boffins, you know, in DEFRA. Aint got a clue why they so agitated about cod, and not bothered at all about turbot and brill.

The Fight To Change The Quotas

We go to the meetings with 'em, and we try and get our side across to them, but they don't take a lot of notice of 'em. I've been to a lot of meetings in London in the past few years and that but you sit there and you could bang your head on the table. You don't get nowhere; you really don't. All they're worried about is getting rid of the fishermen because, Simon Doggard, he used to work for DEFRA and DEFRA run politicians now, they run the big boys. You know all the over tens, ten metre boats, they run it. Three years ago we was talking about quota again of course, and we aint got no quota and he said, "What we do, you've got your quota, what we'll do, diminish the fleets to meet the quota". And we've got three thousand five hundred boats I think it was we got, all the way round Britain, and he says he'll diminish them to eight hundred boats, to meet the quota. That was three years ago and we've got it all in black and white, all on the minutes: ridiculous. This is a bloke now who's, well, probably sitting in a higher class job 'cause he got moved on; terrible, terrible. Paul's (Joy) had three days in Brussels, fighting our cause, but where are we getting? This meeting tomorrow: we got Conservatives coming down tomorrow and that, and a lot of the people from around the coast or in NUTFA, that's the new one we've set up in the East Hastings Angling Club. They will all be there as well so we'll see how that goes tomorrow. DEFRA won't be allowed there. Its all to do with this new, what were going to have, Conservative government if they win we're getting in to it now, and there's a lot of people coming from all around the country. Amber Rudd, she'll be there'll be a lot of other people I don't know nothing about. Paul says there's going to be three tables: the head table for obviously the top class people. There's going to be another table for us fishermen type of thing, and another table for anybody who wants to be there. Michael Foster, I admire that man because he's spoken on our behalf many times, but unfortunately we still got nowhere. And he is the Labour candidate of course, and he spoke very, very well for our lads when they had a problem with court cases, and got them off of it, and he's always backing us up, but we don't seem to get anywhere. We haven't got anywhere at all. The minister Hugh Davies, the Welsh chappie, he gave us 70% of the quota, to start with then he changed his mind the next day 'cause DEFRA got hold of him, on the big boys side, you know.

I think a fair system should be for the amount of workers there are in the either, the over tens and the under tens. I think the under tens have actually got more workers than what the over tens have, more actual, members, but it don't work out that way because they get far more'n what we do anyhow. Fifty-fifty would be alright but he did say we'd get 70% of the quota in this area, but that all come to a no-no. Fifty-fifty would be great for us. Area7d, which is off our coast, stretching all the way across to France and as far as Dungeness down to the Isle o' Wight, I think it's, I think there's 23, 24 registered big boats, you know, over tens, not all from here. Well, actually the quota system gives people in the Northern Isles, up in Scotland: three or four places in Scotland, Northern Ireland, they've all got quota here, in the Channel in area 7d; they never come and catch it.

They've got the quota so they'll lease the quota out to you or I if we want to buy it off 'em, you know, so, this is what it's all about now, leasing. But don't don't quote me on everything to perfection, cause I'm only saying exactly what I know and what I can remember.

John 'Tush' Hamilton

26th of May 1942

Family And Fishing History

My name is Tush Hamilton; Tush is a nickname, my real name is John. I was born on the 26th of May 1942. Our family were evacuated to Wolverhampton, so I arrived back in Hastings when I was about three or four years old. I'm not going to introduce myself as a fisherman, although I done a few years fishing in my very early days, most of my life has been spent on what we call the other side of the Stade which is selling fish. My Father was also involved in selling fish and he was one of the very many fish hawkers who were around in the early days.

Hawkers

My earliest memory of this was probably at the age of about seven years old I would think, when the fishmarket was at the bottom of High Street across the road where the amusement park is now, and I can remember going down there at that age helping my Dad on the market. In those days, unlike today, that's now finished with, but in those early days there was an auction, so the auction started at something about quarter to six or sometimes about five o' clock in the morning, and I worked up a little business down there because in those days there weren't many fridges around but the Hawkers used to keep their fish with ice; right opposite the

Hastings Fishermen's museum was the Ice House and I used to come along to the Ice House about half past six, seven o'clock in the morning to collect ice for the Fish Hawkers, and they would give me a penny, or a penny a' penny in those days but it amounted to, four or five pence which was quite good for someone the age of seven years old; so in those days my Dad was one of the many fish hawkers.

Now a fish hawker was a guy that pushed a barra. He would buy fresh fish on the market and push a barra to various places in the town. Some of these guys had pitches and some had rounds. The difference was if you had a pitch and some, one fella I understand had a pitch by what was then the cricket ground, he would push his barra there everyday and he was allowed to stand there from eight o'clock in the morning until around twelve. My Father had a round. Now my Dad wasn't allowed to stop, he used to push around the houses and shout out what he had. So for instance if it was the herring season he might be shouting "All landed, just landed, fresh herrings, sprats" and the people would come to his barrow with their plates, he would weigh the fish up and they would take it away on their plates and move onto the next house, or the next person that come out, and my Dad would have had about three of these rounds, I know, I can remember one of them being Stonefield Road area, because nobody would go there because it was so hilly, I've been many occasions with him walking around with this barra and by about eleven or twelve o'clock they would sell out and then come back to the fish market and wash down ready for the next day.

Now hawkers would go out five days a week probably Monday, Tuesday, Wednesday, maybe Friday and Saturday, and a hawker would only take what was landed locally. Now by that, in those days there weren't freezers around or there certainly weren't many, and the fish that would have been sold on my Fathers' barra would be what was landed that day, or the day before, the night before. So he would of had maybe only three, four varieties of fish and unlike today in those days people would eat what was in season, so if it was in the plaice season he would sell loads of plaice and dab's and if it was the herring season it would be herring or mackerel in the mackerel season; people ate what was in season. Now the shops in the old Hastings and there were quite a few of them too, some of them, some, sort of about eight or ten fish shops in the Old Town up to, sort of St Leonard's. Now they would have a much better variety because some fish was transported to Hastings from London market on a train, and that was picked up about six in the morning and taken to Hastings market. Now that could've come right from as far as Scotland even, and that would travel down in the day and arrive in Hastings in the early hours of the morning. So from that you would get skate and haddock, or what was ever in season, in the area it had come from, could've been Scotland it could've been Lowestoft or on the East Coast, it used to come from everywhere – quite big business really, and people would go up, one chap had a truck, a big old lorry, go up and collect dab's every morning and then that was distributed, but mostly shops we used to have, hawkers had normally gone by the time that had arrived and, as I was saying they only took , local caught fish. As the years went on I obviously grew up and I first done a bit of fishing when I was about sixteen or seventeen years old and I quite enjoyed it.

I worked with an old fellow called Oxo Richardson who's now dead, he was quite a character in the Old Town and I had about a year with 'im. I then had several trips with Charlie Haste who was a trawler man. But it wasn't long before I saved up enough money and bought myself, well a very big rowing boat in those days with an out-board and believe it or not you could get a living with a rowing boat and out-board in those days. So for the next few years I used that until I eventually ended up with what we call today punts – an open boat with a diesel engine, and I worked that on and off, not every year, sometimes the winters were so bad I hauled the boat up and went to work, but I worked that through the summer up until just before I got married.

Taking Over Hart's Shop

I worked on many different jobs; building firms. I worked in a fish and chip shop, I always worked, and I could always manage to get work somewhere and when I eventually became engaged to get married, I couldn't see any future in this fishing, it was hit and miss in them days we would earn one week and not the next, and although my father had told me many years to go the other side of the Stade selling 'em, I did like fishing, I was very interested in it, but eventually I done just that. I sold the boat, and we bought, and I say we, my wife Pat and I, we bought the oldest fishmongers in Hastings which was then run by the Hart family and it was up in High Street, not far from the museum in High Street.

That was around about '67 I think, about 1966 or '67. So I would've been then about twenty-four or five years old. Anyway I knew nothing about selling fish. I remember going with my Dad but, the old boy what run the shop, he run it with his sister, Jack and Rose Hart and they'd had that shop in the family for nearly a hundred years when we bought it. I learnt the trade of fish curing which was done in those days much different than it's done today; today it's all done by mechanical kilns, mostly run by computers, so it's quite easy but when I done it, I was taught to do it the old fashioned way, and the fish was hung in a thing called a Dees and what it looked like was a little bit like the net sheds that are outside the museum, but it was built in brick, and each side there were racks and you could walk up the side o' this place like a ladder, and then my wife would hand the fish in and we used to hang it on the racks and then light a fire built of Oak logs, as soon as the fire was alight, use Oak sawdust, damp the sawdust down so that it smouldered and that's how the fish was smoked. Depending on the weather, cod probably from start to finish took no more than about six or seven hours, five or six hours maybe, herrings sometimes twenty-four hours.

We used to do Kippers and Bloaters. Kippers and Bloaters are made out of producing Herrings, and a Kipper as you probably know is split open, that used to be brined in a very, very strong sort of brine and hung up to dry and then it went in the Dees, and then that was smoked for perhaps six or seven hours. The Bloater was a different thing, all the scales had to be taken off and they were dry-salted. Now they were put in for a number of hours in dry salts, when the time was right they would come out of the salt, be washed and they were all thread along sticks which were called 'spits'. You used to get eighteen onto each spit and then maybe I would hang twenty stone – a stone is fourteen pounds, around about six point three kilos today. But we would put about twenty stone of these in the Dees and set the fire alight, soon as it was ready damp it down with the sawdust, and these had to be turned about every four or five hours, so even through the day and night many a time I've called my wife out of bed at three o'clock in the morning to come down and give me a hand to turn them, because we could turn twenty stone in ten minutes, on my own it would take me two hours because I had to bring each one out and then go back for a bit, but I could wedge myself up in there, hand them down to Pat, she would then hand them back and I put 'em, we turned the whole lot round. When I say turn 'em I mean take the racks that were at the top of the Dees and bring 'em down the bottom, I'd take the bottom ones up to the top. So they all got the smoke; quite a job, it didn't have to be too hot, if it was too hot you could cook the herrings and then they were of no use at all, and believe it or not we never had a temperature gauge, it's unbelievable really what I'm gonna tell you. There were no lights in the Dees for obvious reasons, the bulbs would black up, there were about four candle lights in there, and when I was working through the night I would light the candles, and go in there and you could see quite well with the candles, later on I had to put a mask on, at one time I used to go in there without coughing and choking with the smoke but once the fire was lit we never had a temperature gauge; there was an iron bar that hung down from the ceiling,

John 'Tush' Hamilton removing herrings after smoking them in his deeze.

and the only way I knew whether that fire was right was by holding that bar, and it took quite a long time to get used to that. I could tell by that bar whether the temperature was right, and the door was kept open by a seven pound weight which we used to move, maybe have it open only an inch or two inches or four inches, whichever it was all down to weather conditions. And we had a terrific name and we sold many, many, many hundreds of smoked fish.

I have no idea, why it was called a Herring Deeze: it was used for smoking all sorts of fish, I mean we done everything, it was actually called a Herring Dees. I really don't know why, it wasn't called a kiln it was a Dees, the fire was a log fire which was, which was made up on a steel plate cause the concrete floor would'a been about six foot by eight I suppose and that steel plate we used to move the fire around on the concrete. Because again you didn't want the heat in one place all the time, so in the very first part of smoking that fire might be moved every hour, put one end and then put the other end, then in the middle.

The Dees was just behind Hart's and when we took that over it was the only one left; I understand some years before there were several up All Saints Street, but that was the only one left and we were licensed by the Herring Industry Board which was quite a thing, you know they used to obviously check the kippers to see they were done right and we were given a license, or Jack was given a license which was passed onto me. There are none of them left now, they're all finished, we worked that shop for about twenty years, in the end it got too much work, too many hours involved, I mean it was a seven day a week job, night and day, it wasn't a job, it was your life, and I s'pose, well I loved every minute of it in there, but in the end it just got too much, I just couldn't handle it, none of my children, although they've all got their own jobs now and they're all doing very well, none of them were really interested in it and to be honest with you if you're not interested in the fish game don't join it, because to get up at two or three o'clock in the morning, bitterly cold weather, believe me you've gotta love it.

Lifeboat

Well again, right from a very, very young boy, in those days there weren't the rules and regulations there was today. I always can remember out in the lifeboat: I only used to live in George Street and when the lifeboat boom went off, I mean I don't know how old I was, maybe nine or ten years old. My Father was in the lifeboat so it was just natural for me to run over and help the boat out, and we used to pull it out in them days. There were no tractors, when I was involved there were no horses, they had horses many years before, but we literally used to pull that boat out, there used to be about twenty people each side and a rope attached to the trailer that the boat was on because in those days the lifeboat house was right by the boating lake, right by the road today and it used to have to be pulled out of that shed right along to the end of boating lake opposite the Albion and then pushed right across to the beach and launched there.

To get to the Lifeboat use to take twenty minutes, not that long really because all the help lived around the Old Town, they were all there in five minutes. I mean the crew would've been there before that y'know, they would've put all their gear aboard and it was literally pulled straight, when everything was ready, it was pulled straight out the shed and launched. She was called 'Cyril and Lillian Bishop'

I remember the new one coming which was called the M.T.C I can't remember what year that was, but not many years, how long? Must've been about 1950 something, is when they built the new lifeboat house which is where the one is today although it was a lot smaller, and I think the M.T.C lifeboat came there, but it was still pulled out by hand then, and that went on, right up 'til we had the new one which was an Oakley boat called 'Fairlight' that was designed to be launched off of a carriage. Now I'd been involved with that boat ever since I can remember. I was also what they called a jump in hand.

Well jump in hands were, when I was one, there were about four of us who were launchers of the lifeboat and when you became about, in those days, sixteen or seventeen years old, if they were short-handed the old coxswain would lean over and pick one, two or three of you to go in the boat 'cause in those days there was only about eight crew. My earliest memory of the coxswain was George Moon so I don't know quite when it, what date that was, but I remember being called aboard and really was unbelievable to be asked aboard. "Go and get some gear on youngun" they used to say. Gor, dear I'll never forget going, especially the first time.

My father was on the Lifeboat for many years and my dad actually was in ones that they rowed along with oars. I suppose I had about five or six years of being a jump in hand. I had many trips with many different coxswains to and the thing was with jump in hands, they normally became the crew after a couple or three years, somebody would leave and they would take one of the hands in and that happened to me when Joe Adams phoned me up to go down to the office and see him, Joe Adams being a fish salesman also the secretary for the lifeboats for many years, and I went down to see him, he said "Tush look, we've been talking and the crew want you to go on the lifeboat as crew". Well I was gob-smacked because at that time nobody knew what I was doing, but I was just in the process of buying Hart's fish shop. I hadn't told anyone because y'know s'been going on, been going on for a few weeks; I'd been trying to arrange money. Anyway I had to tell Joe Adams, so I said "Joe I can't do it, I can't, y'know if this comes off I can't be away from that shop" there was only me and Pat then, we hadn't long been married and there was just no way that I could've got a call and gone, 'cause in those days a trip in the lifeboat could end-up four or five hours unlike today; I mean it's so fast today you have these trips about two hours I think now, but in those days it wasn't, it was always six or seven, eight, ten hours, twenty hours even. So I had to sort o' tell 'im and I was really gob-smacked about that 'cause I really would've loved to 'ave done it. Anyway I couldn't do it and it was about a year afterwards when they had a tractor come with the carriage. I might be getting this slightly wrong I'm gonna re-cap with this a bit. We had the 'Fairlight' with the tractor and I was still a jump in hand then, that's right and I think that Joe Martin was the skipper in those days. Then the tractor driver left, or was going somewhere else and they asked me if I would like to do the tractor, which I did because I knew then that I'd only be away from the shop maybe only quarter of an hour at the very most. So I took that on which I done for about thirty years and when I became sixty I had to come off of that and I then became what's known as the Head Launcher and finished my days of that when I was sixty-five. In all I think I done forty-four years on the books. That means from the time that you're actually signed-on by the institution, but I'd been there ever since I was nine or ten years old.

One of the first memorable trips I had was with Jack Edmunds who was the coxswain, George Moon was a coxswain I think Bill Martin was a coxswain then I believe it was Jack Edmunds. Anyway Jack loved Rum and aboard the boat in those days there was always either Brandy or there was a spirit because it was so cold, and they were allowed to have a drink after, I don't know, maybe a couple of hours at sea but my first memory of Jack, we'd been called out to a yacht that was in trouble down off of Rye Harbour and I'll never forget it as long as I live, we jumped aboard "Get aboard youngun'" he said, old Jack, lovely fella, like Friar Tuck one of the nicest men I think I've ever known. Anyway we hadn't got round Rock-a-Nore, and out come the Rum bottle well, I mean this Rum was like treacle, now they poured it out in cups and believe me you got half a cup. Well I'd never tasted anything like it, I didn't know what to do, no way I could drink it. I couldn't throw it away in front of everyone, but they was all drinking this Rum because it was very cold some of the winter nights in that boat. But anyway I did have couple of sips and at the appropriate time when I never see 'em, and when she hit the sea I just threw it out the cup. I just couldn't drink this Rum. But Jack was known for it he loved Rum and as sure as you had trip, as soon as you was out the harbour the Rum was brought out, don't matter if it was in the summer's night.

I've had some lovely trips really, I mean I some many nice trips with Joe Martin, I liked Joe Martin very much, and I know we went out once for one of our own fishing boats that had nets 'round propeller. Lovely calm night, old Nobby Terril and that was quite an experience too, 'cause they had all their nets out and they had net 'round the propeller so they was having a job to haul the nets, so we literally had to, well they put Men aboard the boat to try and get the Herring nets in course these Herring nets would've been about probably half a mile long, before they could tow the boat in but it was calm, it was a lovely calm night that was one thing I remember. And then I remember having a trip with Freddie White. That was when I was driving the tractor, I don't why I went, maybe it was, normally my trips with Joe Martin was when I was driving the tractor but he would only ever call me on a calm day, if they were short handed, because he said when it's rough I want you on that tractor. So I was lucky really, I never had too many rough trips.

Mine

I think the last trip I remember quite plainly was with Freddie White when he was coxswain. One of the Newhaven beam trawlers had got a mine in the trawl and we had to take out the bomb disposal people, that was quite an experience we went alongside the trawler, took the crew off and put these two guys from the bomb disposal people in the boat, and that had to deal with this mine, it was actually hanging over the side, so they had to go in the water in Frogman's outfits to deal with this mine and when the time came they called the lifeboat back – we took them off and they detonated that mine. We were told to steer clear two miles and the trawler and when the mine went off a terrific explosion, although you couldn't feel much, you felt the boat shake and the water came up, the water board up all brown, from the sea bed obviously and all fish floating around. I remember it stunned all these fish; you could go 'round and pick the fish up. And I spoke to the bomb disposal guy and said it didn't make such a bang as I thought, he said it would've done if you'd 'a been ashore, and if you'd 'a been ashore, cause it was right off of the sky-scraper, and he said if you was in the top of that sky-scraper, that would've shook the windows. He said the sound travels along the sea bed and along, and then up buildings.

Rescue

I had quite a long time, well I mean we did have the one really bad launch was when I was driving the tractor, everybody got commended for that – I think Joe got a gold medal. That was for the rescue of the 'Simon Peter'. I think that was about 1976 or something, in the winter time there was terrible bad weather, about force 10, and this boat fishing boat from Rye was actually stemming the sea, couldn't turn 'round. He was trying to turn 'round because you would've gone over, so all he could do was just put the boat in gear and keep stemming the sea and he ended up right up off Hastings and the boat was called out about eight o'clock in the morning, been all night out there. And it was unbelievable, terrible, you couldn't see the harbour, and when we walked down Joe said "We better go and have a look at this, do you think we're gonna get away with it?" Because it wasn't an easy task to launch the lifeboat, it was high water which meant that the sea was right up under the bank. We couldn't afford to make any mistakes; otherwise the boat would've gone off the carriage and washed ashore.

Anyway we looked at it, we stood down there for about ten minutes actually, trying to eye-up where we were gonna go and in the end he went for it he said "Are you happy?" I said "Yeah, let's go for it Joe" and we did, and we were on top of that bank I would think for another twenty minutes before we actually took the plunge to launch the boat and when she went he was so delighted that she'd gone away, I remember he threw his hat up in the air and it ended up in the water. But anyway you couldn't see that boat after the first couple of minutes, as she went 'round the wall, nobody could see her, in fact we was quite worried. I remember we was all on the beach trying to look for this boat but because of the sea, eventually we did see her when she was about quarter of a mile out and they took the hands off of that boat and brought 'em back to shore, and that was nearly as bad getting back ashore, because that was low water time and they anchored the boat and miraculously the boat was still there in the morning, so it had been out there for about forty-eight hours in this weather.

When I say stemming, well it means that they weren't going, they weren't steaming into the sea, they were just literally holding her head into the sea. I mean it was south-westerly as far as I remember; south-westerly and westerly, so they were actually just holding her head into the wind Ie what they were frightened of, if they tried to turn 'round, the sea would've rolled 'em over Ie it was so bad, and that's what they done, and they done that right the way up to, I think our boat picked 'em up about two miles out, up off of Bexhill somewhere. So they been doing that all night, it must've been terribly frightening but, yeah that's really the worst time that I've ever known for that lifeboat to go to sea.

Oxo Richardson

Oh Oxo, what a character what an old character he was! Friend of mine since I was a little kid, and I can remember Stan, he used to have a barra again like I said my Dad was a hawker, they had these wooden carts with wooden wheels and Oxo had one of those, and he would collect various different fish off of the fishing boats; I mean he would have all different sorts displayed on this cart and by the old fish market, which was at the bottom of High Street as I said earlier on, he had a pitch there and through the summer months he would pick up each one of these fish and tell the tourists, they would all stand 'round the cart, he would tell 'em all about the fish, how it was caught, what it was, where it was, how it lived, all about the fish and then he had collecting boxes 'round the side and people would put money in and he got a good living from doing that all through the summer, and then in the winter he would go fishing. An' he was known as the 'Herring King' because he had, as far as I know, he had one of the biggest catches of Herrings ever landed in an open boat in Hastings. I'm not sure, the exact weight but somewhere's about five or six hundred stone, and that night I was Herring catching in my boat, and I can remember as plain as yesterday It was so calm, it was really, really calm, like a mirror, and we'd been pulling our nets in and Oxo came steaming in and all you could see, it looked like he was standing on the water because the boat was so low in the water, in fact I would say that it was no more than about six inches out the water. If it hadn't been calm he wouldn't have been able to do it, but he pulled all the nets in, he steamed past us, we couldn't believe it, never seen a sight like it, and they were all night shaking those Herrings out and when the stack of Herrings was on the market you would just never believe that all that lot of Herrings came out of that boat: And we were only half a mile away from 'em, we had sixty stone, so it was his night, but he was quite a character.

He had the wonders of the deep. I kept on to him to do it in the latter years and he wouldn't do it and then one time I said to him "Well if you don't do it, I'm gonna do it" because I still 'ad one of these wooden carts and his words were "You won't be able to do it like me" I said "Well there you are, you come and do it " so we done it between us for the carnival and collected a lot of money, and it was then that we decided to try and bring it back and I said I'd help him because in today we 'ad fridges so we could keep all the different kinds of fish and we did try it but one of the downfalls was the fish cost a fortune: it cost well over a £100 to put that fish on the tray and it only lasted two or three days and unlike in the days when he done it, Squid and Cuttlefish and Tope, these fish were thrown away but today they fetch a lot of money. I remember we paid £34 for a Conger Eel once, to put on the barra; in the old days they were literally thrown away. So it just wasn't viable, we tried it all the year but it just didn't pay, so you know we couldn't do it.

The Fishmarket

The market where I started I was on that market with my Dad, my Father used to work on that market in the Fifties, when they built the new market I think. That was a terrible, terrible old building.

So that was really where I first started buying fish. Now in those days there was, I think about fifteen or sixteen trawlers and quite a lot of punts. Now the fish in them days was auctioned. The fish would be stacked, there were two concrete slabs, long concrete slabs 'bout thirty foot long and about six foot wide, and the fish was stacked on them in the order that the fish came in. For instance; if RX2 came in, he would push his fish up, and his stack would be the first stack and the next boat that landed would go the other side. As these boats landed, they stacked their fish all in order and it was sold in order. Joe Adams then had two set of scales, one on each slab and he would sit in the middle of these slabs with his book and he would auction first the right-hand side boat, then the left-hand side boat, then the right-hand side next boat, then the left-hand side next boat.

So as they landed they were sold. That was very important in them days because there was so much fish, the very early boats were first off selling, and very often they got a better price, and the last boat sometimes ended up going to wholesalers which meant that they got very bad prices. So sometimes the boats would actually come ashore for a turn, and I've actually seen them stick ashore and put a box of fish over the side and the boy-ashore run up to the market to get that turn before they unloaded.

And then, this was in the very early days as I say, just after the market was built. As years went on fish became less and that didn't seem to matter so much then because there were a lot of hawkers and there also became a lot of wholesalers on the market in the Sixties, and so it wasn't that important to get a turn because they were in battle against each other, the hawkers and the wholesalers. But it was the very fairest, and I still say today although some people don't agree, it's the only way to sell fish, by auctioning it because it was so fair. The fishermen got the price that fish was worth. Now I can tell you that if I was short of fish, if the weather'd been bad for a few days and then it calmed away and boats went, I wanted fish for my shop and I didn't really care how much it cost to get it. Yes, once I had a stock then I could stand back and let the prices come down. So those fish always fetched the price it was worth. Obviously if there was loads of fish we could stand around, it was our fish market then, it was our market. I would buy fish cheap, so it was swings and roundabouts and definitely in my opinion and I still say today the ruination of the fish market was when they stopped the auction in about, I would think about nineteen ninety something. I don't know why they done it, I really don't know.

Well it obviously was the fishermen's decision to do it. I don't really know,I mean they must've all decided to get a guy in from Newhaven, who was gonna take this fish, rather than auction it; he was gonna take the lot, which he did do for about seven or eight years, but I used to then buy from that guy so the boat landed to that guy, he then sorted it and graded it and we could buy from him and he would sell to any fish shop and then he would send it to London or wherever he sent it. He became the middle man and prices went up because they had no control over the price, he determined the price by what he got for it, so he sent that fish to where say for instance he did used to send the fish to London, to the West Country to all over the place, but I don't ever know how they determined the price of it. And again in the old days when the auction was there, if you looked after your fish, I'm talking about fishermen now; if they gutted it and washed it properly and graded it properly they got better money, because we knew the boats that looked after the fish and if you were, as I was and I was known to be a very, very fussy buyer and there was a lot like me who wanted the best, and I paid to get the best.

But once it went into this, I don't know what you would call it, into this wholesaler, it was too late. All the fish was graded so whether it was of good quality or medium-grade quality, if it was a pound sized fish it all went in one box, or boxes. So I don't see how that could ever been better, but this is what they thought was as better to them. Now, whether any one of these people who ever'll miss it I don't know, but it's gone, that went on for about eight years I think, eight or ten I can't remember and then that guy finished. I don't know the full story and I don't want to implicate myself to say what happened but he finished, I don't really know what happened. And then I think, it was then that the market in my opinion then really started to fall apart because boats then started selling their fish wherever they could and some sent their fish to Newhaven, some sent their fish to Rye.

It's not graded anymore, now we have the company they call the C.I.C, the fishermen's own company, and now I don't know how well this is doing or what, but I do know that the fish now comes in and then the C.I.C company people grade that fish and send that to wherever they send it, but as I say I can't comment on whether that's good or bad, but that's what they do now.

Now some of the fishermen don't sell to that company; some of them sell to Rye, some of them might, I'm not sure; I think some of them still sell to Newhaven.

Everyone's fish in my opinion should've gone on the market and be sold, an' the only way to do it, is by auction. Now I said this to a guy not long ago, but he said to me "But it's finished now, it would never work" now maybe it wouldn't work now, it's too late now, maybe it wouldn't work, I don't know. Maybe you'd never ever get the buyers back. There was all sorts of buyers there: there was people like me that run shops, there was people in vans that bought fish and went to London and sold it, there were wholesalers, there were people that worked with cod, y'know that sort of particularly bought cod, there were the people that particularly dealt in dover soles; so you had all sorts of people, I mean at one time there would be thirty or forty people 'round that auction, and all battlin' for their own fish. As I said if there was tons of fish then the prices would come down, but if there wasn't much fish…

I was in Belgium the other week and they've got an auction there, unlike the auction that we used to have with Joe standing there with the prices – this is how it's worked: the hawkers or the buyers view the fish and they sit in a room and there's a big dial on the wall and they've all got sort of like a computer type thing I suppose, and then in the room the guy will say for instance whatever boat is gonna be sold and we say, "We're selling these plaice grade one first" and then the price will go 'round on this dial and when it hits you wanna pay you press your button and it's yours – and that's how that auction works.

I was also down in Bristol that's still done a little bit like Joe used to do it, but the fish is graded again it comes in on the boats and it's graded by people in the fish market by graders, and each boat is laid on the floor and the auctioneer will walk and sell that boat, then walk to the next one. Much the same as Joe done it, but it's still auctioned, and it's still auctioned I believe in many, many of the big ports. So, whether or not it would work I really wouldn't like to say now, but in my honest opinion it's the only way for fish to be sold, and that's what I think.

Well we'd been in there (Harts) nearly twenty years so it was bout '96 or something I don't know quite when it was, and we'd then decided to sell and it was bought by a guy who unfortunately, he run it for a couple of years an' I don't know what 'appened there he got fed up or something and it eventually closed down, which was a terrible shame really. I think he had it for about three years and it closed down and yeah, no more fish shops and yet y'know there were one or two in All Saints Street, there was us in the High Street, there was quite a few but when we closed it I then decided to go, well actually I wasn't gonna have nothing to do with fish in the first instance, but then after a few weeks of being out of work I realised I didn't know much else about anything else. So I then decided to buy a van and do markets. Well at that time my mate had got one market and it was too much work for him, so he asked me if I'd go in with him, which I did and we picked-up a couple of free, nice markets all 'round South London, one in Cranley, Walton-on-Thames. Anyway, we picked-up some good markets, and I worked that; there was still plenty of fish around. Sometimes I had to go to Rye to top-up, but mostly was local caught, mostly, and I would prepare it, I mean that was my job so I was pretty quick at filleting an' that. So I would buy the fish on Monday and we would go out and sell it Tuesday, I'd buy the fish on Wednesday, we'd go to sell it Friday, and then we would again buy fish on Friday, and go and sell Saturday. So that was how we worked this van and we built up a lovely trade because some of the fish that was sold to some of these markets in London was only a few hours old; fish that they hadn't really had I think. And also amongst that we picked-up quite a number of restaurants around South London, so we used to do them as well. Then my old mate became ill and he had to pack up, and then I worked it, well I had my wife with me for a little while but it was such a long hours, although less days it was long hours, it was a one o'clock start in the mornings till about six o'clock at night y'know?

So in the end I sort of said to Pat "Look I don't think you should do this job" And I then got some more help and Pat went to work for a Doctor. Anyway I run that for about, must 'ave been about seventeen or eighteen years I think, and then in the end the same thing, I was gettin' older, I couldn't 'andle the drive, I couldn't 'andle the hours. So I decided to out that, so I sold it. So in all I 'ad over forty years selling fish, one way or another.

Fish Rolls

Then when we sold, it was when the Fish Roll thing come about, is the thing that we still do today and I'm now 67 years old, I still do it with my wife Pat and we still enjoy doing it. I mean this Fish Roll thing come around by: we'd always cooked fish in a big frying pan up in the garden when we had barbecues and my neighbour Graham, one of the fishermen, he used to do the meat and I used to do the fish. Anyway we'd done this for many years and one week Rick Stein was filming down on one of the fishing boats, I think it was on Paul's boat actually, Paul Joy's. And they done their filming and they arrived ashore about twelve o'clock and had a few hours to spare before they went to their next venue. Anyway Paul at that time was 'aving a barbecue, Graham and myself up home, and Paul rung-up Graham and said "We've just come ashore can we bring Rick Stein up? Is Tush cooking fish?", "Yeah." "Was it all right to bring Rick Stein Up?", "Yeah fine!" Anyway Rick Stein being the old fish cook on the television, he came up and was quite took by what we were doing with this fish. Simple cooking and fish that he hadn't never actually heard of, one of the fish we were cooking were Gurnard, we call 'em 'Gurnets' the red fish full of bones. Anyway we were cooking them and he literally had never seen this done, and he tasted 'em and he asked if he could film us which he did do, and after he'd filmed us cooking this, I mean they all sat down and ate it, we had a few drinks in the bar and they moved on to their next venue. They were doing a series around the coast. Anyway two or three weeks afterwards this lady rung-up his secretary or PA or whatever you call these and asked if Rick could use this bit of film in 'is series, so we said "Yeah fine, don't mind, no problem." And he did, so what happened there, it went on the television.

Well the next thing is we got a phone call from the Hastings Council would we go 'round with the tourist team cooking local fish y'know, to help with the promoting Hastings and the fishing fleet, so yeah, why not? We'd never done this before to the public, we'd only ever done it in the garden. Anyway, believe it or not our very first venue was Belgium, so I was a little bit nervous of doing that, but we done it, and it was a terrific hit and we've been there now, I think this was the eighth year we've been to Belgium. But since doing that we'd been all 'round with 'em, in the early years we'd been to Portsmouth, right up as far as Liverpool; all over the place doing this fish with the Council and built-up quite a nice little earner really, but unfortunately it ended up with about four shows, and there wasn't enough there to warrant runnin' the fridge, and refrigerated vans and everything and my wife said to me "Why don't we do these fish in a roll and sell it at boot fairs?". "Boot Fairs?" I said "Who's gonna eat fish in a roll?" "Y'know people eat burgers at boot fairs, I think it would work" and me knowing everything said it wouldn't! Anyway the following year the shows nearly dried up, we only done two next year, one in Belgium and one in Portsmouth or somewhere, so there was no point in keeping all these fridge's running, so she said "I think it will work", "Okay you think it will work, we'll try it but it's got to be on the beach, we can't do at boot sales, it won't work, it might work on the beach, we'll try it!" So I came along and saw my friend in the museum the man I am talking to now, Phil Ornsby. I picked out a couple of places where I thought it might work and one of the best places, I thought was the half boat which was owned by the museum, anyway I spoke to Phil, he put the wheels in motion and it went to the top people, and we got a letter to say they were quite happy for us to do it, they thought it would be a good advert, you know for the museum as well, so we tried it, and it was a bit of a hit and miss thing, a bit of pickle on a wooden table we had, we tried it in September of that year and it looked like it was going to work, so from then on we've built ourselves a nice little rig out and today we still work on that museum, we donate a few bob to the museum, and do a few bits and pieces for them, we're very grateful to be there, they seem to enjoy us being there.

And so we do that, and we still do the shows for the council and a few others too, we've just done the last one actually now it's the end of our season so we've just finished now and we've built up quite a good trade for these rolls...

John 'Tush' Hamilton smoking herring in his deeze.

PAUL JOY

23rd of October 1949

Family History

I was born 23rd October 1949, so coming up to my sixtieth year. I've been in the fishing industry for about 39 years I believe now. I was born in Hastings, I've come from a long generation of fishing families; in fact they go back to about the twelve hundreds or so. Well actually some of the evidence we've had that it was back here to the ten hundreds. So, we've really been here for an awful long time and always fished from Hastings, effectively generation after generation have fished from this area, and as Joys, it had an 'e' on the end but then so did many words in them days.

I've got a younger sister and an older brother by two years and two sons, my brother was allowed to come into the fishing industry: he went directly into fishing and he's been there ever since. He had a period where it was very quiet. In the early days we went lug digging to make up his money but he was always generally in the fishing industry. Obviously my sister wouldn't go into fishing, so left me in a round about route to actually come back into it because initially my father wouldn't let me come into the industry. He said I had to get a proper job, couldn't become a fisherman like him. So I started off and went into horticulture through the local government training scheme and went to Horticulture College. Once I got my passes what I needed then I went into building, landscaping for a very short period of time and then the chap I met on the building wanted to go fishing and he bought my dad out and I went fishing with him as a crew and then my dad worked as a boy ashore then for the boat and me and then I bought him out and ended up in the same position where my father was anyway: In the same place. So it was round in a circle and in the end my dad was very pleased that I'd come back fishing. We acquired several boats over that period of time, bought another boat, a bigger boat and on to the boat I've got today. and we've fished successfully for a little while now a few years, up until the advent of the restrictions which have come on to the Coastal communities, through the UK, as a whole.

Will Joy, my dad, was fishing prior to going to the Navy. Most of the brothers volunteered in the 2nd World War and they all wen' in for the big adventure of going to the 2nd World War; and after the war they come out the navy; they went back into fishing. The brothers all fished together lots of arguing between 'em, they was always falling out and fighting, and in the latter stages it ended up, 'Booty' or Percy Joy and dad fishing together in the 'Fairlight Bell' and then after the 'Fairlight Bell' they had a new one built called the 'Mara' and they fished with the 'Mara' two handed, sometimes three depending on which one fell out at the time. Jim and Dick were still mucking about fishing and Jim then decided to go on the Local Authority Council and he went on the Parks and Gardens Department and he stayed there then, he didn't go back fishing. Dick, Uncle Dick, he went fishing; he had a little boat built called the 'Vilma', and he went on fishing from there with Rod, and the son Leon is still fishing today.

His friend was Major Eves and he was a barrister and he drew up the '47 Deed of Compromise. There was 44 vessels and 44 stades, and the council tried to evict the fleet and move them to Rye; they wanted the fleet completely removed and put all the fishing fleet into Rye and The Deed of Compromise was drew up in '47 and then from there the fishermen still have the irrevocable license for the ground still in place today.

Fishing History

He fished using a small open boat; it was the 'Mara' which was a 19 foot open punt with a eight and a half horsepower Lister engine and we used to have a foresail which helped when the wind was in the right direction; and that's also the boat which I fished from in my early days when my dad was retired. Willy would have caught the same, basically, as we catch now. It's from three main species, cod, plaice and sole but also made up of other species, turbot, brill and lemon sole and dog fish, fish we're not allowed to catch today, there were no restrictions; you were allowed to go out when you want, catch what you want and hence the good days. I started fishing in 1970/71; I know that because I've got paintings from Laetitia Yhap where I was fitting up nets on the beach. So that's 41 years. First off, I went as a crew for the RX89 which was a punt which Terry Haddon bought off my dad. Terry was a builder who wanted to go fishing for a living, he was fed up with building. I then bought partnership with him and I started off as crew then I bought in a partnership with him and his agreement was if we had another boat he'd allow me to become half owner. I then come half owner with the RX264 then bought him out and then I had the RX83 after the 264 and now I've got the RX89 which was strangely enough my dad's original boat when he finished fishing so I've got the same registration in the family that we had with me dads' little boat the 'Mara'.

I had periods where I needed to supplement my income; we were classified as full time and we was told that we couldn't do any other job apart from fishing, but we had periods where you can't get to sea for six weeks from bad weather and sometimes I jumped on and helped somebody, anything to make a few bob to supplement the income; same as anybody would do. The wife had to be paid at the end of the week! In the seventies it was totally different than it is now, the only

Paul Joy and Ken Moss on the RX83 'Sandra'.

problem you had to contend with was the weather conditions. There was no such thing as quotas or management system. You had an open fishery, you was allowed to go out there and catch what you liked.

Fish Regulations

I think it's in excess of thirty years now that Ken has crewed for me; he's over thirty years with me now. We're basically catching the same as my dad was. The difficulty is what we're allowed to land, one of the problems today, like spurdog is a prohibited species so they all have to be discarded and unfortunately the quota system means we have to discard many, many prime fish which we catch today. Cuttle fish now constitute my main source of income for the year; I probably earn more on cuttle fish than I do for the rest of the year on all other species which has become in the last two years a very important precious stock species. There were restrictions on sizes, we had Sussex Sea Fisheries sizes and you also had legislative sizes from national government, from DEFRA. So for instance, today, I can land a turbot as big as a postage stamp; up until a few years ago it was thirteen inches was the minimum landed size and this was brought in by European directives as a conservation bill believe it or not. There's many sizes have been taken off on fish today, which we are totally against, to allow them to be caught by member states. Lemon sole and many others have no size limit on that fish. Why I don't know. I don't believe it's feasible to pull this on a conservation bill which was sent through Brussels to allow member states so they didn't discard too much fish but as they don't have a swim bladder, flat fish, and they are very hardy, very strong, you keep 'em out water for hours, throw it back in the sea and it'll live, so I don't understand the legislation being passed or allowed to be passed but it's votes in Europe are counted by each country. Britain has six, France has six and so on. Some countries have four and it was outvoted, Britain opposed it and it was pushed through, France, Spain, Holland, Belgium, they all passed it through: they wanted to be able to land smaller fish. The culture of fish eating on the continent is different from us, as most people are aware. You can go even today, which is 2006, we can get to a point where you can walk over to France and you can see small dover sole maybe a few inches long on the quay for sale. Now it's ten inch is the legal size under European law but the enforcement might be a different thing altogether in some countries than others, and you look at Spain, the culture is to have more small fish as opposed to one large fish. Where our culture, we would like one big fish for a pound, the French would buy four for a pound 'cause they prefer the smaller fish, but it does nothing for the ecology of the system if you take the juveniles out before they have spawned.

So, it's a cultural thing, it's also an economic thing. The quota problem with cod at the moment is partly a European problem but it is, in essence it's a British government problem because the way the quotas that are allotted to this country have been split up. Each year the member states are allocated a section of fish, a lump of fish and then that is shared, or should be shared proportionately and fairly by each member state. Now, each member state adopts it's own system how to manage it's own quota, from Europe. In some countries they have ITQs, which are Individual Transferable Quotas, which can be transferred about. We adopted in this country for FQA's, Fixed Quota Allocations. The problem being with fixed quota allocations in this country, we had a divide in the industry in the early days, in '87 we got to a point they split the fleet into half, over ten metre, and under ten metre but they said to the over ten metre boats, "You can buy an acquired quota, and you can form Producer Organisations to manage your quota effectively. You small boats, it doesn't matter about you because all we require is estimates, under European law for you and therefore you can't buy an acquired quota and you can't form PO's; we will manage your quota through a government pool." In essence what accumulated over a period of years is that the pool was given all to the big boats who could then buy an accumulated quota and if you look at nationally, today, 97% of the vessels in the UK are small boats and yet 97% of the quota is owned by the big boats, in essence we have 2% of quota for the small boats, and 1% for the non sector, which is another thing, which is little bit difficult to explain, but you've got 97% of the quota is now in the hands of the big boys, and yet we make up the highest proportion of vessels and man power in the UK.

We fish in an area divided from Hythe Bay to the Isle of Wight, which is classified as area 7d. In that area, 93% of the vessels are under 10 metre, and 86% of the work force, but we've actually got about 29% of the quota. So, it doesn't equate. You've only got 20 odd vessels over ten metre who have all the quota, basically. If you take 7d, there's a quota for each breed of fish, for a year. You have a yearly quota, but it's actually broken into monthly allocations: for instance cod is a winter fishery for us and we can avoid catching it in the summer if we don't go down into deep water, so our cod season will go from September 'til April, basically and we can't avoid catching cod in that period because it's so prevalent and also the method we use, of netting, don't matter what type of selective netting we use, we will always catch some cod. So, effectively we cannot avoid catching cod during the winter period, so our quota should be set during the winter period. Our problem comes today, where the quota was allocated to the big boats and left us with none to fish on and we are sitting back here having to dump fish, simply because the quota has been given to the wrong sector of the industry.

We're not allowed to catch them because we are under ten metre boats but the larger than 10 metre boats never ever caught the cod. They even admit, the people who have got the quota on cod, now admit that they never caught it. They've been given it and if you was to look on, it's now assimilated into what they call producer organisations, the big boys sector. Now, our quota for cod here, in the English Channel, 7d, is in the Outer Hebrides, Shetland Islands, Aberdeen producer organisation, Northern Ireland, South West, and Cornish POs, they hold bulk of our fish. If we want to fish on our own fish, we must rent it back off them 'cause they've been given it. They can't catch it, they never catch it; the only way they can do anything with it is to allow it to be rented. Let's go back fifteen years: I could buy cod at £25 per ton, if I was allowed. They're now renting it at a £1000 a ton. So it's a big money making organisation. It's about profit, it's about big business. Today we've got the situation where the Producer Organisations, dominate and control the fishing industry of this country and dictate policy and unfortunately if we want to fish we must rent our own fish back off them. It seems hard to believe but that's an actual fact.

France is a prime example of how to work the system: for instance we got France and us in the Channel, Belgium, but if you look on the division of quota in our area, 7d, half France really, it's half England, 76.4% of the quota goes to France, 8% for England. So, there you have a situation, the beginning of the demise of the British fishing industry, you never got a fair share in proportion to the vessels that actually worked and then being under ten metre, in our area, South East makes up the largest population of under ten metres anywhere in the country so you was already disproportionably allocated quota because no one bothered to ask what we caught, and even though we gave them figures over the years, they was ignored and they wasn't used as a bargaining tool to get a fair percentage of quota when we went into Europe. That's the beginning of the problem; they've escalated since, obviously from the other manner which I said they allowing quotas really absorbed into one pool, and not in the other.

There is a fishing limit in the Channel of six miles for us and France is the same and then you got sort of international waters between. There is occasionally encroaching but to be perfectly honest the problems we have are not in that respect, our main problems are trying to get to a point where we don't dump fish, which is another scenario which is part of the problem we've inherited because of lack of quota. If you look up to 2006 how we worked during the winter period as a fishery up to then, cod I took on a personal level made 40 to 65% of my income over a year. Now it doesn't equate to 3%, because I'm not allowed to catch it but saying that, we're discarding more cod than we've ever caught. We've tried to make many, many governments and ministers understand that we've always fished in an environment friendly manner: we get to the winter period, I would move my mesh size from four inches on sole up to, 150 millimetres, 160, 170, even a 180 millimetre net. Then I would fish for cod. That means I would be very selective, I don't have discards, and I would only catch a cod in 180 millimetre mesh, at about twenty pound and above but if I catch one cod a net, I can sustain the family, I can sustain my crew, and we can sustain jobs as little as that and it means we have no discards, but the government in it's wisdom now says "Look, you got quota on sole, go out and catch sole." We explain to them that sole migrate to deep water in the winter, "We can't catch sole, it's not here. We have to catch what we can." They said, "No, you go and fish on sole." So effectively then we got 100 millimetre mesh in, and now instead of catching the odd large cod, I'm now catching cod of just over landing size, right the way through the spectrum, up until the large. So I'm discarding far more than if I actually fish for it. Now this isn't conservation, and it has nothing to do with the sensible attributes to learning how to fish, and look after a community, it has nothing to do with it at all but, because we're small coastal community fisheries, and we're small boats and we have no quota, we have no voice. We have no voice in decision making processes; we're excluded from the processes that actually make the decisions on our behalf and these are set up with things such as Regional Advisory Councils. Everyone who sits on a Regional Advisory Council which is member states, so you've got Britain, Europe, France all the member states, sitting to decide fisheries policy, there isn't one small boat from England that sits on any PO. No representative, nobody. Every single member is a PO executive who are The Producer Organisations, even though we make up the numbers.

Fish Seasons

We're now at the point where the sole season is pretty much finished but still catching a few plaice and we've had a little mussel bed, we're picking up a few, but they migrate off very soon, within any time now, we'll be on cod nothing but cod. I actually gave this scenario when mixed fishing and avoiding catching cod what percentage was cod if he was to go out every day for a week to a group in Brussels, Green Peace and WWF and I made this point exactly: you've got 339 vessels here in 7d under ten metre on the registry. You got 300 that work in Poole, in roughly the same area, from the Poole registry. So you could have about 600 vessels working here, all can't land one cod. Now, let's say I could land a ton a day, cod. Effectively I could land a ton a day at the moment, that's trying to avoid it. Now, let's be realistic,

Paul Joy and Ken Moss clearing nets on the RX83 'Sandra'.

and say I call it a week, I mean even if you called it a month, and you only land, discarded a ton a month, 600 ton thrown back in the sea, dead, a month, at a very, very, very conservative estimate. No one's interested because we don't have quota. It therefore doesn't matter, and we think it does, because we're destroying our own fish stocks, 'cause we're not allowed to fish in a sustainable manner, we can't fish any cod.

We formed a national organisation; it's called NUTFA which is the New Under Ten Fishermen's Association, to take the government to court for judicial review. We had 400 boats affiliated to our association; at the moment I'm the joint chair. There's three thousand and fifty under ten metre boats out there and we've got four hundred. Members who are strong enough to pool together to fight for government fair play. The trouble with our industry is it's always been fragmented and that's the trouble we've joined as a unit form here, because we have a strong association, but you go into another Port even Rye for instance, we've got five members in Rye, and the rest are all backing us 100% but they won't put the money in. It's putting money in to fight is a different thing. When we formed this organisation each member has to put some money in to become a member of that organisation which is a fighting fund. It's basically because we all work for free, no one's paid; all the directors of the association are voluntary, no one gets paid for anything, so we spend a lot of our own time, our own effort travelling around the country and Brussels etc. to try and fight our case and promote the cause of the inshore sector. But it's very difficult to do when you've also got a full time job as a fisherman. Most of us are in the same position; my counterpart, joint chair, is Dave Cuthbert from the South West, fisherman, same age as my self, who's as vocal as myself. He fishes out of Plymouth it's the second in proportion to numbers, the South West. There's a lot of South West boats but they're going fast. We are losing boats by bankruptcy as opposed to any other method. They brought in a two tier licence system, to try and eradicate all the vessels down and looking at historic catch landings that didn't work because you just register your boat under a devolved administration and then there's nothing they could do about it. For instance, at Hastings we have Richard Reeds' boat RX59. It's now registered under the Cardiff registry, CF instead of RX. So it's now a Cardiff boat now fishing at Hastings where, and he's had to do that to be able to get a quota to fish on because he was laid up during the reference period because he couldn't get a crew for his boat, they've stripped his licence away and said, "Sorry chaps, now go bankrupt!"

They also had decommissioning, and they spent a hundred and twenty million pound decommissioning the over ten metre fleet but also told them that they could keep their quota. So you've spent a hundred and twenty million on decommissioning big boats, and told them, by the way, keep your fish, where the government could have brought that fish back in, with the boats they decommissioned, and reallocated it fairly, if they'd wanted to. The chances have been there to do it, but they didn't take the opportunity of doing it. I can give you an example, Peter Leach, Shoreham: he's got two rusted old beam trawlers, not even two years ago he decommissioned these two old boats, 1.6 million they gave him and they said, "Ooh by the way keep your quota." So he got 1.6 million pound and he bought four smaller beamers; now they are devastating our ground, they can tow up to the shore, they are very powerful, and this is what they're meant to be progress.

The answer is to strengthen the association, and this is something we've been trying to do in the last few weeks, we need a full time paid executive to run round and do our courses. It needs someone who is articulate, can be passionate about what he believes in, and also smart and eloquent enough to stand up to the big boys of the industry. We need someone who can actually say, "We're sticking up for the small coastal communities and the sustainable communities!" and this is what we're really trying to do at the moment. But it's a step in the right direction we've had European Union last week myself, Gerry Percy and Dave Cuthbert to give a presentation on a European summit and the next day we was asked to speak at the World Summit, and we went down very, very well. We actually got standing ovations and people were shaking our hand and WWF and Oceans Twelve, Greenpeace, were all coming up and saying "Yes, you're absolutely right. This is the way of the future; you should be looking after coastal communities that are sustainable": but you've got to get past your own government. You've got Europe saying come over and speak 'cause this is what we want to hear, we've got our government on this side saying, "We're not interested in you, we just want to wipe you lot out and give the fish to the big boys."

What I was very interested to hear was the Catalonian Fishermen come up, and obviously and the Spanish said, "Oh by the way, we don't actually put some of our small boats into the quota management system. We exempt them, because they're environmentally friendly fisheries and they're small artisan fisheries." Now we come exactly in that category, then why aren't we exempted, if we can fish in sustainable manner, on a fish in our area? Now why can't we just opt out that system? That would leave the FQA system in the hands of the big boys. It's because we've been stuck in the common fisheries policy at the moment, and we're in the process of having the reform on the green paper which is come out now. Looking at the European green paper on change from the European parliament, there's lots of changes afoot, and we are going to revamp common fisheries policy. So now is the time, this is the most important time to actually get, a change, to look at European legislation, actually legislating against each state to make sure certain things are in place. And that could be done by having, as I said earlier, stakeholder involvement. Make sure stake holders are, people who actually, in the industry who have a stake in the future. And that's where we could come from by being exempted, but we can't just say, well we've got to come out, let's come out of a system we don't want to be in it. We've got to give alternatives, such as days at sea, increased mesh size, minimum landing sizes, and we're happy to do this.

They've, the European Parliament, admitted at long last, that the common fisheries policy is a disaster and doesn't work. We know that, but on the back of that, we are far worse off than any other member state, and I said to the Commission the other day, "Look, whether I like it or not, I'm a European fisherman, and I might not wanna be, but I am, and I deserve protection, to be able to fish from the European Union." and it's no good saying to each member state, here's your fish each year, and it's up to you then to share it in a fair and proportional manner, you may or may not. It's got to be from the European Commission to legislate to each government to make sure they look after coastal communities because they talk the talk. If you look in The Times a little while ago in the Fishing News, that fisheries minister, Hugh Edgar Davies, he wrote and he said, "It's incumbent upon a fisheries minister to look after sustainable communities and coastal and sustainable fisheries." Now he wrote that and signed up to it, and the next day he took our fish away, the very next day that was in the papers, he took our fish away and gave it to the POs. So, what they say, and what they do is two different things, and we got to have a policy which is actually documented from Brussels, which says, you must do this. Otherwise there is no future for the inshore sector in this country.

PETER KENWARD

5th of August 1945

Family History And Early Life

I were born in Hastings in Fernbank Nursing Home on the 5th of August 1945 and I'm one of fourteen: seven of each! I first went to Red Lake Primary School, which was a pre-school. And then, when I was old enough to go to Infants school I went to All Saints Infants in Harold Road. And from there I went to Clive Vale, and it was split between Clive Vale and Priory Road.

I left school at fourteen and a half, I didn't want to stay the other term until I was fifteen 'cause I was never at school, I was always over at the beach; I was just starting my career but very early! My first job: I worked for a local builder in All Saints Street, labouring: JB Jones, everybody knew 'Jonesy'. In the very early 60's they was building a nuclear power station at Dungeness and I left the building and I went to work on the over-head pylons.

When the construction was finished I came from a very lucrative job to a steady poorly paid job on the over-head lines at Ninfield, working for the CGB which I became a charge-hand there, and they was a redundancy package and I took the money and left. I went long distance lorry driving, and then after that I, thought I'd like to fish full-time.

Fishing

As a school child I was always going to sea with Jimmy 'Toller' and Tommy 'Toller' Adams and always helping the boats up to get fish, and we all had our own rounds and we all had our own customers to go 'round houses selling fish; You'd've got plaice, what we call 'fryers', they was ten for a shilling. We also did most of the best boats which you thought were good fingers ('good fingers' is they rewarded you well.)

I would've been 28 I think: 28 or 29, give or take a year or two when I decided to go to sea. I just enjoyed it and I thought "This is the life for me this free and easy way of life – go when you like, come home when you like." and you forget about the bad weather come Friday, when you share out!

When I went full-time I went with a chap called Barlow on a little boat called the 'Sea Hound' a little punt. Used to pull the nets up by hand, that's before they had net haulers, it's easy now. They put a lot of weather about, you weren't there long really, four/five hours and, there was a mad rush to get the nets done, get 'em back in the water and ashore.

I was the first one to go full time fishing in our family. My dad used to go with the Harffeys, which are a well known family on the beach but they've long gone. Mark Harffey's parents, they had three trawlers I think; The 'Skylark', they bought The 'Dove' off of Tommy Adams and then they had the newer boats built. In the fifties in recent years they had the 'Florence Harffey', 'Two Brothers.' Before that, mum and dad and myself used to go lug digging: my mother was the best lug-digger on the South Coast! That is digging worms out of the sand for fishing. I used to earn a living at lug digging at one time: used to go bait digging on the long tides, used to do two tides a day, that was early mornings, and tea time tides, that's on the long tides; on the shorter tides it was just one tide a day that we'd be able to get down there. We'd have to walk from Winchelsea Beach to Rye Harbour to find any worms and on the long tides used to go here, over Rock a Nore, along under the Glen. Tides used to uncover, you know on the really big tides hundreds of worms, massive great worms there, but it was only like, once a fortnight that happened, if you were lucky. We used to go four or five days a week, but you got wore out if you was doing it seven days a week. Its' also finding a market for them. I used to send mine to Canterbury, to Greenfields at Canterbury. My dad used to drive an East Kent bus and I used to put them on the bus and he used to drop them off. October time there used to be a three day international angling competition, hundreds of people used to come, and I used to earn twenty five, thirty quid as a schoolboy, digging worms. Yeah, it was very lucrative. All the boats on the beach, the big trawlers and the punts, they were all rented out to take anglers, there was hundreds. Where the boating lake is there used to be a big car park where the fishmarket used to be, and everything went on in there. All the weighing in of the fish and everything, it was massive. It was known world wide, people used to come from all over for it, that has now sort of died down I would think because of the weather. They've altered it to June or July I believe now to get the days at sea, but in June and July you haven't got the sort of fish that you would catch in October i.e. cod, and big whiting and that type of thing and I think a lot of it is money. People just can't afford to have three days away to go angling, and then the weather turns bad on them, and it doesn't happen. That is what I feel, why it is dying a natural death.

I had a small boat FE17, which I bought off of Billy 'Ding-Dong' White. Well everybody in Old Town knows 'Ding-Dong': but that was a failure, lack of money, lack of experience. We sold that, but I went to sea in one of Graham Coglan's Punts with Stuart Bartlet – pulling trammel nets up by hand and that was quite good, that was brilliant. My first boat would've been about 1980, '81/'82 somethin' like that, might even been a little bit later than that. I went to sea with Graham Coglan in what was Tom Adams's boat, The 'Lorraine Carol', RX16. Went with 'im for three years. I went to look at another boat, I couldn't afford it and I told him about it, he said "Ohhh, I don't want that." The next thing you knew he'd bought it! So I said "I'll buy the other one off of you." which was very, very successful. Graham Coglan had changed the name to 'Daybreak'. I had that for a few years but it was really old, very leaky and I saw the 'Golden Sovereign' advertised. I found it in Chichester harbour; I went down and looked at it. It was unmarked hadn't been used professionally for very long and it was ten years old when I bought it. I brought it back to Hastings and several people said, "You won't get that about on the beach." but I did. It was heavier than most of them and it was a deeper draft. It was built at Eridge near Tunbridge Wells, a chap called Stan Curd built it and brought it to Rye, and then put it in the river and then fitted it out there. It was built for Dungeness beach but not very successful. I got that Golden Sovereign in '83 I believe. We had that for several years, until such time as I sold it.

The end of the beach I was on wasn't the best end of the beach. Up at the harbour arm they would get off in a breeze, but along this end where the sea would just be bigger swells. I was the last one to the East, and it wasn't very kind for getting off. Yeah it was bloody awful, coming and going and I just had enough of it, and bought a different boat and went to Rye, which was much easier: just step on the

RX40 Golden Sovereign.

boat and sail down the river. I think it all works about the same because there's an hour sometimes, in them days, to get the boat to the water, and then pulling it up. It's no different you weren't away from home any longer, going to Rye. A lot of people have left the beach at Hastings, gone to Rye, even these days. Rye fish market is not a Dutch auction like it used to be at Hastings: that was the best auction around. You could come ashore, with your fish, you put it on the market, you say to the auctioneer, "Oh, could you make my money up please," and that would be ready as soon as he's finished the market he'd make the money up. You got a list, who's bought it, what weight, how much it's made. These days, where it's just a price, you get your money and your ticket at the end of the week, you don't know who's bought your fish but you've just got a set price and that's it; if you produced a good product, you got top money for it: if you put crap fish on the market you didn't get very good money for it. Their Rye fish market is very similar to what they operate here now; the wholesaler sells it, he's got all his clients what he sells it to, a lot is exported, and then he stops a percentage. Takes the expenses out of that for his handling and transport and all the other bits and pieces that go along with it, and then you get the rest. Back in the eighties there were quite a few boats in Rye there was still more here in Hastings 'cause you had all the punts and that; at one stage, you couldn't walk between the boats from one end to the other. There was that many boats on the beach. Obviously a lot of them have fell by the wayside now, where there's not that interest in young lads coming into it. They prefer to get a job where they earn regular money, (it's so hit and miss in the fishing) even if you lose half of these, the ones that are left there, they'll survive, it's just the nature of the job now, they diversify. They go rock hopping, that is having a trawl with a big foot rope on where they go on really rough ground. They go triple rig trawling like they do now with three nets on the back of the boat. Herring, scalloping, they do everything now, they have to. Myself, I did mainly trawling all the time. I did do trammel netting but you have to get involved with making nets and having a crew. Half the time they don't want to go so I used to go on me own, so I had crews from time to time till they got fed up but a lot of them days they used to go fishing for cuttle fish but with trammel nets with a bigger mesh in them, and they done well, until the traps come along and they do even better.

In Hastings you got a lot of help: we had a normal boy-ashore to help pull up and push off, before we started using bulldozers. Jimmy Read was the boy-ashore then at the time. Derek Ryder, he was boy-ashore for quite a long time but they didn't like it because we had a lot of wood to get it up and down with, which is hard work, especially when you've got to pull 'em, down by hand but now you just hook it on the bulldozer away you go, it's easy. The shingle became high after storms made banks and links what we called them. About ten or twelve of us used to have a wooden plough it's like several scaffold boards and handles on it and we put it on the winch and then pulled it down the beach, and the winch pulled it up the beach, pulling about a ton of stones up at one time, and used to level the Stade out.

There's always the maintenance on the boat when the weather's too rough to go out, there's the servicing of the engine, greasing up of the winch, mending the nets, we used to have to make new ground ropes, that's the first part is contact with the sea bed. Also, there's the trows to make, a trow is a three foot six long piece of wood, fifteen inches wide, and with an inch and a half inset in it which is called a saddle, which keeps the boat in the middle of the wood. There's those to make, periodically, because they wear out, and they get lost, so there's always something to do. There's fish boxes to make, in the old days, they were wooden boxes, used to have to paint them, wire them round to stop them splitting, and put your name on 'em, and put handles on them. There's loads to do.

We'd just have a, thurrowed haul which was about 20/30 stone an' that. As we "Chuck it in Bob for one more, just a short one while we pick this up and have a cup of tea". Well, that didn't happen, we'd just started pickin'-up after about fifteen/ twenty minutes the wires went together I said, "We'd better get it up Bob". We had, I don't know 80/100 stone for about twenty minutes, the best catch I ever had of plaice. We come home and we pulled the boat up right on the road and somebody said "Oh Kenward's got trouble". Peter White, who was over there, he said "Yeah he's got trouble alright, he's full up with plaice! That's what trouble he's got." and that was our best catch and we made in excess of four figures for that trip. That was back in '83. I still got the ticket in-doors now: but that doesn't happen like that every day.

We had one catch, one day, it was the last haul of the day. We was only fishing just under Fairlight Cliff. I thought "Time to get the net up" and we used to pull it over the stern then. I said to my mate Tony, "We've got something quite heavy here!" because the net was going back to the bottom again, if it's a bag of fish it just floats to the top. Having winched it in and it come on board what dropped out of the net was this bloody great bomb! Turned out to be a thousand pound American bomb which made you rather tight lipped in all directions, but we just put it back on the sea bed, in a safe area what we thought and the bomb disposal people came the following day and blew it up, which went up with a quite a bang! We'd already taken the fish out of the net, couldn't leave that behind!

Majority of time we went to Rye Bay but it would depend on what time of the year and what amount of time you had, i.e. whether you had a tide either six or seven hours or whether you was having a full trip, 12 hours plus but because the ground is kinder to the gear, up in what we call up inside here it's all pretty hard and it's pretty mercenary on the trawl. You know, you have a lot of mending to do all the time, but the quality of the fish, just in off Hastings, is superb, really, really good fish there's more in Rye Bay but generally it's smaller; there's more boats in Rye Bay. Where them days it was, you'd have to jockey for position to go down to the, what they call the' hole in the sand' 45 minutes South East from here, that's the west end of the hole. That's when you first start, but if you was about last away you would steam east so you got in front of the pack or you'd go, what we called out over on the white land, that would be like five miles out, five and a half, whichever piece of ground you was fishing on you was going down through and p'raps you was the first, you would go where you want to go. A lot of them, they would come up in the opposite direction, they would either edge you in, or edge you out and eventually you don't get where you want to go, so to save all that hassle used to go somewhere completely different, and be on your own, which is easier. And in those days you didn't have the tractor to push you off used to be a days work before you got to sea, and sometimes a bloody sore back and if you didn't help one or two of the others you never got off yourself, and everybody had to help everybody else. Maybe you didn't want to, but if you didn't you never got to sea yourself but it's easier with the tractors these days, but I think boats are not made to push from the front, and I think they do suffer on the wear and tear, to be honest.

I had two further boats in Rye; one called the "Echo" which was a 30 foot boat, and then I bought a bigger one, 35 footer, after that called "My Lads" One was steel, and the latter one was fibre glass, which are good sea boats, you don't have to do a lot of maintenance on fibre glass boats, they were good., plus the fact they don't leak at all, you know you get the wooden ones bounce about on the beach, they leak a lot.

Packing Up

I didn't plan to pack up fishing, I went to Sunderland to buy a bigger boat for Rye: it didn't happen, I came home the next day and that was on the Friday. On the Saturday I went to the Angling Club and chap said to me "Dave wants to sell his shop." and I came down on the Sunday morning and within a couple or three hours we'd agreed a price and shook hands and that was that and we're here now. We're in our sixth year this doesn't rock and roll about at all, once you lock the door up, that's it. With a boat you gotta come down, has the water come far up round the boat? Is it going to jam up under the railings at Rye?…and all that. I don't miss that at all, done my share.

Having good local fish that's what we've built a good trade up on. People come from wherever, M25 belt, lot of customers come from up there; they come down once a month, spend a nice bit of money and take home good quality local fish. You know, all the time we can get that we don't buy anything else. I've just finished skinning the skate now as you see, come in this morning, that will be on the counter within an hour we do lovely local bass, wild bass, if they like that. They can't buy that in the supermarket. Well they can buy something that looks like wild bass but it's not, believe me, there's a lot of farmed sold: well all the supermarkets sell farmed bass, and if you look at their fish, it's seen better days. You can smell it. Soon as you go within twenty yards of their counters, you can smell where you are. Fresh fish doesn't smell, it's got its own smell but it doesn't stink.

JACK SIMMONS

18ᵗʰ of April 1935

Family History

I was born in Woods Passage, off All Saints Street 18th of the fourth 1935. We didn't live there long because we was moved up to Bembrook while they were building Hastings Wall, and once they finished we moved down to number eight Hastings Wall and we lived there: apart from going to Somerset when the war was on. I can't remember what year I was evacuated, but I was at school and the whole family went; my father didn't, my mother, my brother, me two sisters, we was all shipped off to Somerset for about a month or so while they was worried about the bombs and that. They had barrage balloons up and all that in Hastings in the Old Town, you know, because they were worried about the Germans coming over.

We came back and I still lived there until me mother moved to number one Hastings Wall because father said he had a better view, he could see the sea better, but that was then. I got married there and then after living there for six months we got a flat, third floor flat opposite the fish market and we lived there for a couple of years. I started school at All Saints school, and then I went over to St Mary's just off the back of where Marks and Spencer's is, there used to be a school: I finished my schooling there.

Fishing Career

I was round about 12 part time fishing with my father on the 'Good Luck', RX100. I used to go with him when I had a chance to, you know, until I left school at 15 then I went on the 'Enterprise', as a half share hand, picking up and gutting the fish for a couple of years I would think. I was on a half share because there was so much fish that people had to take on a third hand, so I was a third hand with Harold Pepper, who was the owner, and his brother which was Stan Pepper who finished up to be my best man.

After that I took my first skipper's job which was on the 'Little Mayflower' RX106 and my crew was Wilfie Adams, who's just died. They was my crew and I fished out for about three years, I think. Then Stan Pepper boat was laid up because it was leaking so much he got a boat in Rye and he asked me to go over and work with him. So I worked with him on the 'Johns Model' RX 178 and we used to travel to and fro. It got a bit much travelling to and fro so I moved over by doing a council exchange. We did a swap with a man who had a council house in Rye and we did a swap with our flat to Mr Edwards I think his name was, and we lived there while I fished from Rye. Then after he fished for a while he got a bigger boat, a Scottish built boat, and I got the 'Alexandra', RX87: I skippered that and I had a crew with me called Johnny Button and I took that a sea for a couple of years and then I bought my own boat from Joe Adams. It was called 'The Endeavour', RX18. I think it was built originally to replace 'The Pioneer' that went ashore on Fairlight. So that's the one I bought from Joe Adams, a fish salesman.

That was the first boat that I owned, I had it quite a few years. It had a three cylinder Lister engine in it and after being in Rye I found that wasn't enough power so I took it out and I put a 56 horsepower Ford in it with a 3:1 reduction to give me more thrust. It didn't have a winch to pull all the wires in. It had a capstan you used; or do it by hand. I worked that for a year until I saved up enough money to buy a winch where you just pulled levers and it winds it all in. I worked that on my own for a year and then when I put a winch on it my brother come to sea with me. So I had it twice as easy didn't I?

One time when my brother was with me fishing in Rye Bay our water pump which was in the 'Endeavour', the wooden one, the pump they used to pump the water out got blocked up and he went down there to try and clear it and he got his arm caught round the propeller shaft inside so I had to go to Dungeness power station, you know, and ring my mate who worked there in the inshore lifeboat. It was low

RX18 Endeavour tied up in Rye Harbour.

water and I went over there an' I rung him and he come out in the inshore boat and put me brother in there and he took him ashore and the ambulance took him to Ashford hospital 'cause he broke his arm. But he's alright! Yeah that was one bad time.

As soon as I bought the 'Endeavour' I was fishing at Rye and I moved there. I only came back to Hastings sometimes with the boat to pull it up on the beach to paint it. The 'Endeavour', was a wooden clinker boat. It was 30 feet by 12 feet. I

'Mascot' owned by Jack Simmons, an all concrete boat, the first one built for the Fish Authority.

put a wheelhouse on it. I didn't actually finish with the 'Endeavour'. I decided to get a bigger boat because they had more power, so I bought a boat from Lowestoft from a Mr. Blowers. It was an all concrete boat, the first one they built for the Fish Authority and what they do is that stuff there they make the shape what'll hold it all together like that, and when they're ready they have six or seven men and they plaster it with concrete all in one day. It's wonderful it had a big deck on it you know, wheel house and echo sounder and radar and all the equipment I didn't have. It was called the 'Mascot' RX149. The only bit that's not concrete was the wheelhouse.

Rye

I was in Rye for twenty one years. I preferred Rye because you didn't have to get up and down the beach you just steam up the river and steam out again. The only problem was when it blew hard you couldn't get in on low water, you had to wait till the tide come in. We were dependent on tides at Rye. If it was high water at 12 o'clock you could only get in and out three hours either side, that's going in and coming out. So if you went out at say three o'clock in the morning early and you got out there and had a couple of hauls and it come on to blow hard you had to wait until the tide come in. Sometimes you go on what we call 'have a tide', you go soon as tide come in you go out and have two hauls and come in 'fore it went out. But you could only do that if the weather was right. The idea was to have a 12-hour trip, anyway that's why I went to Rye. If I used to go out at three o'clock in the morning I used to come in at three o'clock in the afternoon you know a 12-hour full trip.

There was a market over there to start with and we used to put the fish in a cold store and they'd sell it the next morning. That's what happened, but towards the end I used to take my fish to Billingsgate market. Now I had a man used to take it up twice a week, Tuesdays and Thursdays but if I went on Friday, on Thursday for Friday's market, I used to have to take it to London in a pickup van I had. I was very friendly with the fish salesman, Freddie Farmer and he used to treat me quite well so I kept in with him but then towards the end of it I come back to Hastings Fishmarket. I used to bring it over from Rye and put it in the Hastings Fishmarket when they still sold it by auction. At Rye market I think you put it there and the auctioneer used to sort of buy most of it in and send it to France, and things like that you know. That's why I started to go into London 'cause I got a better deal at London. Our fish salesman died and the bloke who took over from him wasn't so trustworthy, I couldn't trust him, you know. The fish salesman I was friendly with he was very good to me he was very fair, he was more than fair you know, if I had a bad trip, he used to give me extra money and all like that. But once he died it was, as far as I was concerned it was finished.

Quotas

There weren't quotas when I started. If you wanted to earn more money you put more time in or had more trips. My father wouldn't have understood it, you know, he just couldn't have understood it the fleet at Hastings and Rye they've never over fished anyway so the quota system really isn't working as far as fish conservation is concerned. That's what made me pack up early, that bloody silly quota system from the European market. It's absolutely ridiculous. Two years before I retired, I was catching a lot of cod and plaice in November and December and the quotas come in and said you can't catch plaice and cod in them two months, you can't catch 'em 'til the 1st of January. Well in November and December the cod and the plaice was full of roe, they was in really good condition, right, and you can't catch 'em, you gotta throw 'em back, so one year I even took my boat out the water and painted it in November because I was so frustrated at not being able to catch the fish, this is going back years.

The Simmons

From when I left school to when I finished, I'm 75 and I've been retired 12 years, fishing's all I done, I've never done any other work at all. I got two sons' and a daughter. Both the sons had a go at fishing and they both do realise that it wasn't for them. One said it wasn't enough money and the other one said it was too much hard work! So they both packed up right: One's now been through university and he's got a high paid job and the other one now works for the ministry making bullets so that's that. They only had daughters'; I got three granddaughters, so the Simmons name isn't going to carry on anymore. It's the same in Canada. We got in contact with the people in Canada. My grandfather's brother went to Canada on an exchange on a thing 'cause the fishing died here so he went over there with one of 'em and for some reason something come up about they was trying to contact the family so I got in contact with 'em and I wen' over twice and had two holidays over there. My grandfather's brother who wen' over he had a son but he didn't last long; he had an accident on a tug and he died but his son was named George Henry Simmons. He had a son and two daughters and when I went over there they was fishing from Port Dover and then Bob the son, 'cause like the other, the older chap retired so Bob who was a bloody great bloke he took the boat from Port Dover to Wheatley Ontaria and he used to have five or six Portuguese men doing all the nets and the fish work, he used to sit while they were doing the work. He had a ruddy wonderful life but he died at 53; twice I wen' over there. Once I was over there I wen' a sea with him and see how he did it and he come over here and he had a trip with me in my boat, in the 'Endeavour', and the next time I wen' over he'd died and his wife took me and showed me his gravestone.

Jack Simmons in naval uniform.

'The Good Luck' RX100.

I USED GO TO SEA WITH MY FATHER WHEN I WAS AT SCHOOL IN THE 'GOOD LUCK' RX100 OWNED BY MY GRANDFATHER GEORGE HENRY SIMMONS.

WHEN I LEFT SCHOOL I WENT IN 'THE ENTERPRISE' RX278 FOR ½ SHARE AS THERE WAS SO MUCH FISH TO CATCH.

MY FIRST JOB AS SKIPPER WAS IN THE 'LITTLE MAYFLOWER' AT THE AGE OF 20 YEARS.

I REMEMBER ON THE 1ST APRIL 1949 'THE PIONEER' WENT A GROUND ON FAIRLIGHT ROCKS IN THICK FOG.

ALL HANDS WERE LOST:
SKIPPER HARRY MUGGRIDGE 49 YEARS
JAMES FREDRICK WILLIAMS 27 YEARS
JAMES ATHER HELSDOWN 55 YEARS

THEN ON THE 6TH JAN 1972 THOMAS HENRY ADAMS RX16 45 YEARS OLD WAS KILLED ON BOARD AT SEA

Written by
Jack Henry Simmons
Born 1935

John 'Siddy' Starr

12th of October 1942

Family History

I was born on 12th of October 1942 in Crown Lane in Albert Cottages, which is in the Old Town; I was born at home, not in hospital. I went to school at All Saints Infants School in All Saints Street then from there we went to Harold Road, where there was the All Saints Junior School, then after that went to Priory Road Senior School up at Priory Road. When I actually left school I went to work along at Rock a Nore Road at George Steels place, Rye Arc. I started off preparing stuff for paint spraying, and then eventually I moved on actually to doing paint spraying, and I was there for about eight and a half years. Not what I wanted to do, I wanted either to go fishing which was my main thing, either that or I wanted to go in to the Merchant Navy but because my father died when I was fourteen, I wasn't able to do that because there was only my mother and myself at home and I had to get a job to help keep the home going, so that was it.

Fishing Career

Actually when I started fishing, I used to go to sea with Tommy Adams when I was about twelve year old. I used to go occasionally, not all the time, not permanently, but I used to go fishing with him, and one of the coveted jobs we used to do was, when we was on the shore was to go to the wash house, which was up where the Isobel Blackman Centre is now, on a Saturday, get a bucket of hot water and soap powder, come back, board the boat, chuck everything out the fore room, and scrub it all out. Well we used to do that every week and we used to maybe get five shillings or sometimes three half a crowns, which was seven and sixpence, we used to do very well. Also I mean when you went to sea you used to bring some fish home. We used to eat a lot of fish but before then what I used to do was round September you know, on from there, October, November time when the herring men were actually fishing, I would have been about ten year old, if it was a fine night, we used to nip down Crown Lane, up into Tackleway, to look out to see if the herring men were off there drifting, and if they were I used to go down back home and say to mum, "Herring men are off tonight, can I go over now". So they used to let you go because well and truly everybody knew you on the beach and you was in no danger at all. So over you would go, and stand there waiting for the herring men to come ashore. Which could be anywhere, eight, nine o'clock at night, depending, and you might be standing there up to twelve o'clock at night helping them shake herrings out with the frost settling on you, and the snot running down your face and that's what we used to do, used to help clear the herrings up, box 'em up and then they'd give you a bucket of herrings to take home, so it was more food on the table.

When I first started fishing, I would be working on Seeboard but I packed up because we was lucky enough to have a little bit of money left to us, which I bought a boat and when I first started, I started with Billy Tyrell. Billy Tyrell come to show me the ropes and then from then, he went, somebody else came and a little while afterwards, Jimmy Kent was fishing with us and he fished with us for a long lot of years. And then he went away, then a guy name Michael Booth jumped in for a while. People used to jump in just to try and earn a few pounds like, you know? And then in the end Jimmy came back again so more or less, just before I had to pack up I think Jimmy left for a wee while. Harry Benton was with me then, and then I just had to pack up because the job just knocked me out. The first boat I had was the one I finished in, RX147. 'Sea Jade': All me working life on the beach and every year without fail it was brought up, round about August, and you spent five or six weeks, maybe a bit more having everything done. New planks, dishing it all up: engine and all done up if it needed doing and so on. We used to have maybe two months off, because at the time of the year we didn't have any trawling gear so in the meantime I used to do a bit of hop picking: Used to go out cutting binds at the hop gardens to make ends meet. We were just ordinary netting then we didn't have any trawling gear, 'cause we was only just starting out. Eventually we did make some trawls and get the trawling gear and we would go off on fine nights, obviously it only being a small boat, we carried on from there.

We used to fish most of the time from Pett, beginning of Pett Level up and to Cooden, up that way. But, it depends on whether you might be two, three mile out we never used to go too far, just scratch enough. Fish was a bit more plentiful then.

Not so much large catches trawling we done much better when we could use the trammel nets, which you probably know, they had a fixed net which you leave on the sea bed, and go to and throw, every day really, if you can get to them, but then sometimes you see if you can't get to them you end up with a load of rubbish and then you might lose two or three days cleaning them out, 'fore you can set 'em again.

Fishing Tales

I have several stories to tell: many years ago we used to go off in a row boat, catch a few herrings. This particular night, myself and Paul Joy, just put some five or six brand new nets in the boat, so we went just off the end of the groyne and was drifting up towards the harbour when the inside of the nets started, went round like an L shape, so we thought ah, herrings on the inside. So we decided to drop the end on the boat, go inside and have a look and when we lifted it up all I could say to Paul Joy was "For Christ's sake hurry up and bloody row!" It was a bloody great shark in the end of the net. Frightened us to death it did!! Anyway, so Boris was out there in a bigger boat so we steamed up to him, with Bartlett, he was working with Stewart Bartlett, so we went up to him, said "Bor, we got a shark in our net". He said "I know! We just rolled it out of ours!" So he went in while we hung on his nets and I could hear Boris laughing, anyway, Stewart said, "Bloody thing!. It was almost as long as the boat," he said, and we was pulling on this net, this bloody great eye come up out the water, anyway, busted through the net and off it went.

We've had one or two close misses with the sea coming aboard 'cause of the weather: come up on us too quick, it could sneak up on us, and we was just about to start coming home and the sea peeled off went over the side of the boat, it knocked Jimmy off his feet and all the diesel went flying everywhere. All we could do normally with a situation like that, you put the head of the boat into it, we couldn't turn so we had to put our bum to the sea and pump like mad. We had two electric pumps and a hand pump and that's what we had to do, and we had to gradually, when we were emptying out, gradually edge our way home. But we was four mile out at the time so we could have gone down in one fell swoop, so I suppose we were lucky to get back. But these things happen unfortunately.

I'll just hop back quickly to when we first started fishing. As I said, when we first started Billy Tyrell and one or two of the others came with us. In those days, we couldn't work an awful lot of net, maybe twenty nets, basic, per time, because we used to have to haul them up by hand. Well if they were full of weed, I mean it was a struggle to pull the damn things up and there used to be a lot of sea urchins and such like, well, those little pins on the sea urchins used to break off into your hands, sea mice, which also have spines on, you'd catch your hands on them, and by the time you finished, your hands used to be throbbing like mad. Used to go home, have a drop of warm water in the sink with some Dettol in, and soak your hands and maybe the day, or two days afterwards you'd be popping out the sea mice where they'd gone poison in your fingers. It really used to hurt! We were lucky one year: in the sole season, we made a small fortune as it was then, so then we was able to find the first net hauler for the boat, because they'd just started coming about then, what we called a cotton reel net haulers. So, we earnt enough money to have a good share out between everybody and buy a new net hauler for the boat, so we was under starters orders, then we could start using a little bit more netting. It made it easier when we were trawling because we could pull the gear up with the net hauler. Made it a lot easier for us, so we were very lucky.

Herring Ban

There was a herring ban forty years ago, the first one I think. Just before Christmas, they put another short one on this year, I think some crazy bugger thought, "Well that'll be it." Although you see, you used to have the big fleets, at Hull and all up round that way but most of them was only drifters at times, drifting. Then I think they started seining for them. First seining then trawling for 'em and I think perhaps maybe up that area they were taking too many because then fish finders started coming. There wasn't a shortage, we was doing very well actually, because the fish that you was catching was hooky and we was getting good money for it. Twice the amount as we would have got normal, for less fish, anyway he guy we used to sell fish to, is long gone, so they can't do anything about it, but when you used to walk over the beach in the evening, over the high water bank was a hive of industry. It was all lights under the high water bank and there was all these guys over there with little row boats, one or two had gone in their punts, all shaking out herrings but I think at the time the Fisheries Officer knew what was going on but I think he was

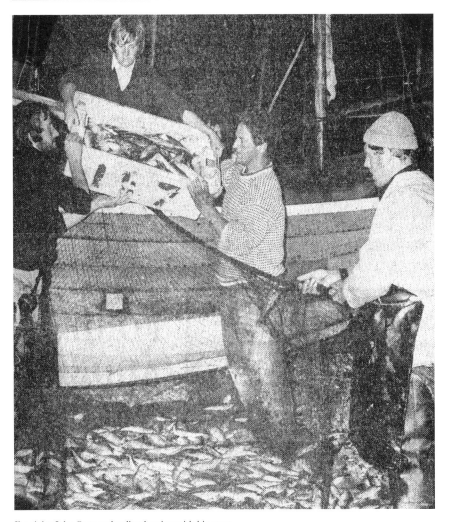

Far right: John Starr unloading herring with his crew.

a gentleman, and all the time it wasn't flaunted in his face, he kept clear, and I was told at one time that one of the guys at the Coastguard, Cassie, I can't remember what his other name was, but he was one of the Coastguards up at Fairlight, and it's been said that he used to ring Cass up, and say to him "Can you see any lights out there tonight Cass?" And Cass would say "I'll just go out and have a look." and he'd probably go outside and have a look and said, "No, there's no lights at all." So, mind you, we wouldn't have been out that far anyway, so he wouldn't have seen 'em, 'cause we was a lot tight in under the shore, and we made some good money. But he did come round one time but I don't know exactly what happened, whether something had been said, but the nets was underneath the row boats, 'cause you turned the row boats upside down, people used to just hide them up. I think he come along and had a patrol along there once or twice but nothing ever happened. I mean, you can't hide herring scales, when they're on the boat they're on the boat, they stand out like sequins all over the boat. But I think, as I say, he was a gentleman. The guy who we used to sell them to used to run them, where he used to take them I don't know, whether he went to Billingsgate or what he done with them. Everybody used to say how good 'cause the money he was paying was, you know, really, really good. It was two, could even be two and half times as what you was getting on the market. Because of the ban, there was a shortage in other places, that's where they went. 'Cause I suppose some were sold as herrings, some was sold as kippers, some was bloaters and so on you see but we made good money out of it. 'Cept that night when we had the shark! Yeah, bloody thing!

Packing Up

I fished for twenty years. Yeah I only had twenty years unfortunately. The job packed me up, I didn't pack the job up, the job packed me up! I just done my back in, it started playing me up and just gradually things kept coming wrong, so in the end I just packed it up. Occasionally I still go down to the beach not so much as I used to. At times I miss it, yeah, sometimes I do, sometimes I don't. When you see these lovely summer days or early mornings, beautiful days and see the guys out you think "Oh I'd quite like to be out there," but just can't do it I wish I could. I'd be more of a liability now anyway, but also, when we were fishing there used to be four or five smaller punts in an area: when the tide was low water and you had to push them out, we used to push five boats out across that sand several times in a week, and then you change tides and you start work two o'clock in the morning; well in the summer time it didn't matter 'cause it was daylight just after three and you take them across the beach when it's at low water, because otherwise you'd have to be laying there all night long. High water would be roughly twelve o'clock at night. That's what I say, if you could go over there, in the winter time, what we used to do is go over about two o'clock in the morning, go afloat when the tide was up and anchor and then when it came daylight we used to row out in the row boat, anchor the row boat up and away we used to go, but in the summer time, we used to work the tides: start early in the morning or as when I say early, as early as you could, where you could get straight afloat and then gradually keep doing that, say, up until certain time, and then you'd have to change tides. You'd have to start pushing 'em, they've got the tractors to push them off now, out across the sand to get afloat say by half past eight in the morning 'cause it wouldn't be high water again till twelve o'clock, eleven o'clock. The big boats used to try, if they could, was to leave them on the bank, so they were ready to go, and what they used to try and do was just chuck down a wee bit, lay the wood, just knock the skid off and hope they run afloat and if they didn't, well they had to wait there, or heave back up and don't go at all sometimes.

I don't know how they used to manage when they was under sail 'cause they must have done the same kind of thing; either that or let 'em go down, put a cable on 'em, and wait till the tide come in say fleet up and away they go, 'cause where they relied on just the wind. But I have been told in the past that fishermen today are not men like they used to be, because I think a lot of the fishermen used to be off there in strong winds and that, be in sailing boats. I think they used to put a lot more into their work. As you know by the boat that's in the museum, The Enterprise RX278 although that had an engine in it at one time, but she was shaped on one of the original luggers. When you've got the capstan there, think that had to be hand wound, you know, nothing to do with the engine, all have to come up by hand, that was a lot of bloody hard work wasn't it? Lot tougher men then! 'Gammy' Mitchell, Georgie Mitchell, well he was a little tough nut he was, I mean, he used to knock a lot of sea about. You'd probably find him off there sometimes when the others wasn't off there, or they was coming home and he was still mucking about out there, old George. They used to say he was quite a tough nut. Yeah, Gammy Mitchell, and 'Quiddy' Mitchell was another one apparently. Some of, the old uns, yeah, bit tough: I suppose they had to be.

'Siddy'

My nickname's 'Siddy' and I can tell you how I got the nickname 'Siddy' : My brother, his name is Sidney William, the old man was William Sidney, so there's seventeen and a half years difference in age between my brother and myself but obviously people who knew him they called me 'Siddy' instead of John. Not many people do call me John, mostly 'Siddy', it just stuck.

The Starrs

My family were builders and decorators, they actually built Starrs Cottages that's where the name comes from there, and The Piece of Cheese, I think there was a wager over that. They couldn't put a building on there and that's why they built it in the shape they did. There were two brothers, I'm not quite sure whether they were great uncles or what they were but I think they had a nice bit of money going for them, and one of them, up and took all the money and cleared off to Canada, this is how I understand it. My grandfather, he was a painter and decorator. My grandmother, she was a big old lady of about thirty stone, she used to sell flowers at the end of George Street but my father, I don't know why, he was a milkman for some reason.

The story that goes that the Piece of Cheese was a funeral directors, they say it was built as a bet, and they made the coffins there. It's been several things. It's been a dwelling, and it's been a tea shop, I don't know if it was ever a cobbler's.

BRIAN STENT

25ʰ of August 1937

Family History

I was born up Old London Road on the 25th of August 1937 in Fernbank. Me childhood was spent nearly all the time over the beach but course in the war the beach and everything was cut off. When the war finished I was eight year old and then it wadn't opened up, I don't know how long I suppose it were 12 month before they took all the barriers down and everything, 'cause at the end of George Street there was a big brick wall and they guarded and everything you couldn't get about and go anywhere but then directly the beach was opened up then we spent all our time over the beach mostly. They fished through the war, course obviously I was only a Herbert, a whippersnapper. They wadn't allowed to be afloat when it was dark. Anything at sea in the dark was classed as an enemy. In the daytime when they come in they had to lower the mast because on the top of West Hill they had the big guns and they used to lower their masts and then everything was all like barbed wire and tank traps and everything. Good job I remember it all little old young 'un, then 'course after that directly you was out of school you was over the beach all the time and when I was a little old young 'un I used to go in a row boat: big old row boats they had then with a chap named Dicky Betts and Jimmy Cooke. Jimmy Cooke he never had no children, him and his wife, lovely people, they lived up Old Saints Street, Ebenezer Road and I was always about with 'im because my father had the pub, he 'ad the Hastings Arms. He went in there when he was 11, come out when he was 66 in the same pub and I was always about with them and funnily enough one morning we come ashore, they all used to do land lining, rowing didn't have no engine or nothing and me mother was over the beach and I thought that's strange, and me nan had died so she come over to get me, I was only a little old lad then. We lived in the pub for twenty one year but I was born in Fernbank which is just up Old London Road there. Then when I come out of there I went to the pub and I lived in the pub for twenty one year 'til I got married. That's all father had done, a publican. His folks, they come from Worthing, when they come down here they moved to the Rising Sun then they left there and dad was just over eleven went into the Hastings Arms. They had a right performance with his step father actually. He got up in the morning, sat on the side of the bed and stood up and must have come over swiney, his head went straight through the mirror in the wardrobe, cut his jugular vein. Time a doctor got up there he bled to death. And then father stayed there 'til he was sixty six and half. Was all he'd done was a publican but he warn't very fit he had very bad feet and warn't a very fit old boy but mother used to look after him, she used to do all the work She was a tough old bugger, mother. My granddad that hung himself, he had a boat, The "Allbrew" RX111 then he worked on 'The Corporation', they used to get the blue boulders from under the cliff for doing the cobbled roads an' that but my uncle said he warn't a nice man. Then three of the uncles they left and one was on the light ship here. One of the boats went out and he was coming by the light ship and they went along side of it and my uncle said "Could you take a bag of washing ashore for me?" he said "I'm gonna be coming off within a few days." Anyway they did that. My Nan was scrubbing the sock, he's left a darning needle in it and it went right in her finger and she went blind from the shock of it. Then me other uncle was in the Navy and there was a lot of trouble: he was a cook and he was somewhere abroad, anyway, he jumped ship and got to Australia, then me other two uncles went out and joined him. And all me relations are out there, but I only know two of 'em they're getting on now, yeah me cousins.

We just had the boy, he's still fishing; he's got four kids. One of 'ems been working down 'ere, me oldest grandson was working 'ere last year for Paul Joy but he's a plumber now. My grandson's had two months helping his father. I don't want him to do fishing, 'cause it's no good now, it's a waste of time. There's so much fish here and there's no boats to catch the fish and they won't allocate you enough to get a decent living and also with the licenses and everything and everyone's against yer, the Green Party, the Friends of the Earth they hate the sight of you if you say you're a trawlerman. You've got so many things against you now. I've had to give my boy a good talking to get fishing out of his sons' mind. I never thought I'd ever have to do that in my life, lovely big old lad he is. He's strong as a bleeding lion and I had to give him a good talking to tell him that when the lad get's back he's got to knuckle down and get his self a job plumbing and forget about boats because it is a waste of time.

RX22 'The Gannet'.

Fishing History

I was about 10 year old was when I first went in the 'Good Luck' with Jack Simmons: he was the skipper and Georgie Mitchell, he was one of the hands and a big chap named Wood. He was about for years he was a relative of Biddy Stonham, Biddy in the tub. Then we used to do the sea weekends, holidays, all the time we was on the beach. Up early in the morning, then do the boxes and in the evening rake the fire out, relay the fire, get the coal, get the water and that was our jobs, and we used to get our money, we used to do it one time for Harold Pepper and then I went with Jimmy Toller's dad and I stayed with them till I left school when I was fifteen but couldn't get a berth as there was 'ardly any boats 'ere then, ended up there was only about nine boats I suppose on the beach. Everything went very quiet like, them years after the war. Then I got a berth when I was sixteen, I was sixteen in the August and I got a berth with Joe Martin in the 'Boy Bob'. Jimmy's dad owned the 'Boy Bob' and the 'Leading Star' and then I went in the 'Boy Bob' for a year but she leaked so bad we 'ad to pack it up and then after that I went in a quite a few boats but then I ended up with Charlie Haste. I went with Harold Pepper I 'ad nearly a year in the 'Edward and Mary' and that's all I've ever done, fishing for fifty year. For a while I did 'jump ins': if somebody was laid up or somebody was gone on drill like doing their naval training then I wen' in.

The 'Breadwinner', I wen' in the 'Mayflower', I wen' in the 'Jessie', all in between times and then I got a berth with Harold Pepper in the 'Edward and Mary'. I was with 'im 15 months I suppose but he was a hard task master, he was like Captain Bligh. And then I left 'im I went in the 'Industry' with Ned Adams he was a lovely man very, very knowledgeable and he had the boat built and she warn't the best of boats for getting up and down the beach and he was a top man when he had a boat previous his uncles boat called The 'Industry' and then he had this one built and it warn't a really nice boat for for the sea or the beach to be honest and then I left him and went with Charlie Haste, he was a good old fishing family: I had nearly four years with Charlie, got married when I was with Charlie and then things wasn't very good.

I was going to have a new boat built and things got right dodgy and Charlie said to me "Well the 'Valiant's' for sale." she was only six and a half years old although she warn't the best of boats like 'cause she was built short, he said "At least you know what you're buying." So I went against having a new one and had the 'Valiant'. She was red and then she started getting going a bit tender on the opposite side where she had the chafers on so I cleaned her all off and I bitumened it black and I painted her black and blue. When she got hit the wife's cousin bought it off of me: Peter Adams, got hit by a ship, and we towed her home stern long all her side was smashed in. George 'Gammie' Mitchell got killed on there. I had the 'Valiant' nine and a half years I then had a new one built I 'ad The 'St. Richard' RX60 built, put 'er on a low loader and took it up to Whitstable and brought her down and then put it in the water, that was the very cold winter we had in 1970 something. The harbour froze over that's the only time in my lifetime I'm 66 now, that I can remember the sea freezing. In 1963 we hadn't been to sea for a couple of weeks nearly easterly wind an' what have yer and snow an' that, bitter cold when we steamed to sea and after we'd been steaming 'bout 20 minutes we started coming into conger eels, the sea was full of 'em all floating dead where the cold had got at 'em. And Bob Tart at Dungeness he had he gaffed 60 odd stone and he sent 'em to London. I thought, well I never seen or experienced it, I didn't suppose they'd be any good, well after days and days when the birds was pecking them they still floated for ages, and Bob that first day he sent 60 odd stone to Billingsgate and got five bob a stone for 'em. We were steaming for 'em, yeah the cold killed 'em.

I bought the the 'Moorhen', she was too big for Rye: 54 feet, drawed ten foot six, ten foot six half and six foot six forward, so I said "I'll bugger off to Plymouth." So I went down there, worked out of Plymouth for nine months, but I lived on the boat, I never lived ashore I used to come home once a month for a few days. Oh yeah I was away, I thought that she (my wife) would like it 'cause we used to go down there on holiday and she used to like it and I thought ah I'll kit her up to stopping down here but she warn't going to have none of it.

The wife come down two or three times and had holidays. One time when I had her dished up I had a new stern bearing and had the propeller done at Dartmouth in the shipyard my wife come down and the boy and my friend and his family and we lived on the boat. We had a weeks holiday on, they was all down there on the boat, but my wife didn't like it down there so I sold the boat and they wanted it brought to Newhaven so I brought the boat back to Newhaven.

I went to Belgium and fished out of there because of my friend, the chap I'd sold the boat and he said "Why don't you come with us for a few trips?" and I ended up six to seven to eight months there. It was cold, well that was a winter, bloody full of snow and ice and one of the Belgium fishing chaps had an accident and when we come ashore I went and got washed up and went up the hospital and met him and the gear had come down on top of him, damaged his back and for a good week it blowed gales and wind easy full of snow and that, and I used to go every day and

Young Brian Stent aged eighteen years aboard RX266 Charles and Robert owned by Charlie Haste.

visit him and take what he wanted 'til his family came over; and we've been bloody good friends for forty odd years or more now. 'The Vicky', was the name of the boat when I went to Zebrugge I loved it. But the thing was I was paying two lots of tax and it warn't really nice on the wife you know, and one morning I left, I got in the taxi to the station and I could see her crying and I thought ah this is going to be my last trip. I loved it; bloody loved it, bloody nice chaps. Used to do for 12 days we was at that particular time working in the North Sea but wen' into Great Yarmouth a couple of times to work on the gear: yeah that was good if you like the sea, 'cause it's day and night. Then after that I bought the 'Akela' then I 'ad that one for over 18 year.

When Tom 'Toller' Adams got killed I warn't interested in being on the beach then, he was me best mate, really was. Well I hurt me leg, see when I had the accident, my leg was very bad and I just really wanted to get away, you know' it really upset me. We was so close, such a good pal and he was such a tough guy I never envisaged anything would ever happen to him, but he got caught with the chain and pulled him in there the winch, (on the side on the winch you can't have no protection: you can't have no guards or nothing) both my wife's uncles, got caught in the winch on the beach, here on the side dolly I was on 'Our Lady' helping them actually and the wife's uncle got his finger caught in the side doll] and he pulled his middle finger off while we was at sea and her other uncle he got his hand caught in the side dolly and he really had a severely bad hand and loads of people have been killed like that because you can't have no protection on there and that's how Tom got caught, there was a shackle in the chain and it got catched and one of his fingers was nearly hanging off; I went to the mortuary, I couldn't believe he was dead and I had a good friend, he was a top policeman and he said "Come on I'll get you up there." And he was in bit of a state but yeah, after that I wanted to get away and I got quite a few friends in Rye anyway 'cause there was a lot of fishermen left Hastings and went to Rye. Stan, big Stan Pepper, young Stan Pepper, Harold Pepper, Jackie Simmons, they was all Hastings people and they wanted to get off the beach. Harold Pepper, he was there for quite a number of years same as over there now there's, there's me nephew and his son, they fish over there, Wayne Butchers he comes from Hastings, he fishes over there, There's Mark Ball and his son, they come from Hastings, they're over there. There's Kenny Butcher's, he originally came from Hastings. There's me, there's my son, and my son's crew, he comes from Hastings; there's most of Rye fleet are Hastings boys. You got a bigger class of boat and you're working out of a harbour. See anytime you can come ashore here, don't matter if you're dead low or up providing you got enough wire on your winch you can come ashore here but not there, you're cut out, you can't get in. The big boats now like my nephew and my friend they draw over 10 feet so they can only sail 'bout hour and three quarters, hour and forty minutes before high tide and they gotta be back by two hours after so they don't get four hours in twelve that they can come and go in Rye but it's a different way of working. There's a lovely quay there now, lovely brand new quay there now and it's a different class of boat.

In Rye what they do, if they were to rely on like cod or plaice or whiting because of the quota system they wouldn't be able to run them boats because you don't get enough quota so from November to May they use a scallop rake, they just go for scallops and then from May to November they just target soles because we got a good quota for soles. If it wasn't for the good quota for soles and catching scallops in the winter, the boats wouldn't be viable because you wouldn't be allowed, you wouldn't be able to catch enough to make the boats pay.

Thirty odd years ago, when we was young, Jack Simmons was working a French fixed toothed dredge. They had a big old boat called 'The Gannet' and they was scalloping there then so we've been scalloping forty odd year. When we used to go to the Channel, when we used to go to the "diamond", you get plenty of scallops in the trawls, the Frenchmen used to go scalloping, like I say they used a fixed toothed dredge which you can only use on something sandy or gritty soil, you can't go on bouldery ground, you can't get where it's stony or boulder. They got spring loaded ones now where the teeth flick to avoid catching the stones or the boulders. The 'St. Richard was only two, three year old when we started scalloping and she's she was built in '69 so what's that forty year back.

I've always done trawling. When I first started when I was full time and when we was young 'uns there was only two full time boats with nets that was Will Joy, that was Paul Joy's father, and his uncle, well was two uncles, Dick just recently died, they was trammel netters and there was the Foster brothers, two old boys lived up by St Clements church and then they never used to leave nets they used to go shoot the nets and lay with 'em or shoot the nets come in then go back out they never used to leave nets down at night and they was all hand made cause it warn't nylon or nothing it was all hemp cotton. In them days there warn't none of this synthetic nylon and polypropylene and all that there warn't, there was only a couple of netters then. And then you'd get like my wife's father, they used to do it in a small boat just shoot a few nets and all that 'cause they were all hand made even the centres like the inners and the outers all hand made, then they used to oil them. All our gear, see a trawl, if you made a trawl you used to preserve it with cutch (a brown dye). Now we use Cuprinol, but then you couldn't let it get near any rusty metal, obviously you use chain for yer weight on the green rope. Well if you stowed it down below anywhere and the rust touched the Cuprinol it'd burn through so you used to cutch 'em. The Frenchmen used Manila twine and they used to use salt peter then they used to use paraffin and tar. But you had to be very careful because you could burn it. If you was using one in the winter it was alright but you wouldn't want a paraffin and tar one in the hot summer weather otherwise it would burn it. Yeah we used to tan it, well you'd only get the 12 month out of a net afore it start going to rot so it was continuous, where you used to make them by hand you'd have a bit of net down the shed and you'd have a bit of net in the front room at home so at night time you'd be making net. When you'd got your time off you'd be in the shed making net then we used to go up fishermen's institute of an evening, all hands used to gather up there and you'd all have your own tack and your own net, making net all the time because it was a continuous cycle they was either wearing out or rotting.

When we fitted the church (now the Hastings Fishermen's Museum) out they said "It'd be a good idea to have a net or something up there over the 'Enterprise' in the museum." so I said "Well I'll go and get one out the shed." and it's been there ever since.

Struggles With Cancer

I still live in Hastings, but my wife died, thirteen years ago last Saturday, 6th of March. Yeah been on me own ever since but five months after she died I ended up with cancer, had it all in me glands, in me neck and that. Then I had treatment for that for a coupla year but that was quite bad, they only give me three to four years if I was lucky and I got over that, but I'd been having treatment for about six months and this 'ere chap I was very friendly with this artist woman, she was a blooming lovely woman in Rye. She lived on a boat and we was friends for years well, with me wife and that and she went and see this missionary chap and he give me, he calls it religious healing, he transmits the love of God into yer. Couple of weeks previous the old doctor was getting worried, he though I'd have to have some serious chemo and I had this healing. I didn't even know he was going to do it, I was sitting in me car, I'd just got round the boat and my son had the boat on the slick in Rye, couldn't believe it and within a fortnight I was back at sea. The doctor at the hospital couldn't believe it and I went with Rick Goodsell, I just went. I said "I've gotta get back at sea." He was three handed so I said "I don't want paying, I just want to get to sea." And then I got better and better and better then I worked with him then he bought another boat for me and him to work. Cor blimey I got cancer come in the neck. So then I had to have another lot of treatment for that. I was at the hospital all the time. I still kept going to sea and all, I was going to sea taking these chemo tablets. Anyway I always suffered with sea sickness. One bleeding time I was coming down to Beachy Head and spewed up all me tablets. I thought this is bleeding handy. I then got over that lot and then it all come back in me head. I had some real serious chemo for that, bloody near died, then I got pneumonia and septicaemia I was right bad. I was in isolation for twenty odd days. Yeah so at the moment it's in remission but he said it will come back but I'll have to wait and see bout that. I've gotta go up the hospital week this Friday and have other tests.

Family Background

How me mum and dad met, my father's stood in George street, by the pub in the doorway and Jack Geering and some others they come walking along and he thought, obviously he knew them, me uncle and me dad and Jack Geering they was all good friends. He said "Come and have a drink." So they had a drink while mother was only 17 and she had a lemonade and what have yer and that's how me dad first started taking a liking to me mother. Well mother was in service to the alderman, he had a big place up the park so one day he said "I hear your courting that chap down the pub." So mother said "Yeah." He said "Well I want you to pack that up," he said "I don't want you going to no-one who's involved with drink. You know what happened to your father." She said "But I love him." He said "I can't help that." So she said "Well I'm afraid I think I'm going to marry him." He said "Well I'll cut you out me will." Well he left a bushel of money which he left to the Dighton fund and the fishermen used to have the interest on it every year. Then when it finished up, there was me, Joe Adams and Barry Connolly 'cause Barry was in partners with Joe years back, he's about the same as me, might be a little older might be twelve month older and we were trustees to it and then there was so much left and then we transferred it over to the Blackman and Lasher Trust and that went in with Isobel Blackman. The great granddads, the Dighton fund, that was just the fishermen, every year, the old one's or the one's that was in trouble used to get so much money every Christmas but that Blackman and Lasher trust I think that was generally not for fishing people but for anybody in the old town.

'Ricky Goodsell'

My mate, Ricky Goodsell, he owns three boats but only through circumstances. He bought one, and then a chap wanted to get rid of his in Newhaven but me mate didn't really want it then in the end, he bought it more or less to help him out, he bought that one, and then he sold one and this fellow up in Scotland, when I went with him after I had the first lot of cancer, we went up to Blythe up on the East coast and we brought a little boat back she was 33 foot, a fibre glass one and me and 'im worked it. And then there was a bloke in Scotland up in Girling, he had a lovely boat it were only a couple of year old, big metal one, but they couldn't make a living

RX60 'St. Richard'.

with it and he wanted a smaller one, so me mate done a business with him. Me and him went to Scotland but I weren't very well when we brought that one back from Scotland. Then, cor blimey a friend, the bloke in Scotland knew this 'ere chap, he was in trouble with this boat up at Scarborough, and he said "Oh Ricky Goodsell he's a good bloke." He said "You wanna phone him." So in the end Ricky said "He keeps phoning up" I said "Well, we'll have to go up and see it." When we got up there, the bloke give him an offer he couldn't refuse so he ended up with three boats, but not intentionally. Well, they're over a £100 a week insurance, it's £40 or £45 to tie it to the quay in Rye, that's before you start.

The Decline of Fishing

They burn a lot of fuel; they're very expensive boats to run so with the quota you wouldn't be able to run 'em. There's only two over ten metres, that's my one which is still there, but he's on what they call days at sea which he's had cut three times, he can only go so many days. He's in the non-sector quota. His quota's worse than an under ten and like I say if it warn't for the scallop rakes between November and May and a good sole quota which they get, I expect that'll be cut afore long, they wouldn't be viable with that type of boat. It's too expensive to run. You're like all the time you gotta have welding done, replacing this and replacing that, very expensive and the metal bellies on the dredge. And it's the same there, I mean, my boy, all through the summer he's night fishing but he does a different type of fishing. He's beam fishing; you go a bit faster so you catch the cod's when they're feeding. He'll catch 'em, his net's not very high off the sea bed with a beam and he catches big cods and all night they chuck 'em over you know, some nights he'll chuck fifty to a hundred back, just terrible. There aint the boats to catch fish now, you've only got a couple of small trawlers up at Lowestoft. Bugger me, you could walk across the harbour on boats in Lowestoft years ago, we used to go up there years back to buy gear. Once a year we'd go up there and stop over night, me and Tom and Stan Pepper, go up in a couple of vans, to buy gear used to phone up and order it all before hand and we would walk on boats, but there aint no boats up there now. I don't think there's one trawler in Ramsgate now. There's no trawler's in Dover, you've only got, about five under ten boats that do trawling and netting in Folkestone. You got a nice fleet in Rye, there's a nice fleet of boats there. Newhaven, there's about half a dozen, used to be bushels of boats there. They are between ten and twelve metres in Shoreham, that's three, and then there's two that work away, they've got five about forty foot in Shoreham. There aint the boats to catch fish now.

I honestly think they wanna get rid of the inshore fleet all together unless they've got something up their sleeve with this EU business because the Poles and the Romanians an' all, they've joined the common market. Well eventually they'll be entitled to have some of this quota, they said they'd never, ever get licenses for the Spaniards in the North Sea but they allocated them licenses. Same as now when people have sold boats or when they've sold licenses, they've been allowed to sell their fishing entitlement, what they've caught over the years they've been selling it. Well that's got into the hands of Spaniards in the North Sea, the Southern North Sea, the Spaniards have got loads of that quota and they've never ever been there. They reckon Tescos own a lot of quota, if that's true I don't know. But a lot of these rich old boys they bought quotas, legitimate, they aint doing nothing wrong and they sit indoors and they lease it out. I'm not educated by a long chalk but you're sitting round a table in Brussels, the Germans don't like yer, the French don't like yer, the Spaniards don't like yer, the Portugese don't like yer: well no one's going to put their hands up to help yer. They'll all put their hands up against yer, you're in a club where you're not very well liked, and like you've got the Germans and the Spaniards dictating this that and the other. It's terrible, you can't win, and they seem to want to make the fleets smaller all the time, they say just decommission it;

we'll get rid of so many boats, trim the fleet down an' all that. Well they've done all that but they're still making regulations and I would of thought now they've had two or three different rounds of decommissioning, I would of thought now they'd be able to say well now you can carry on as normal but every year they make more regulations. I don't know, I don't personally think that they want inshore fishing boats and now you've got, like I say, the Green Party, the Friends of the Earth, everyone's jumped on the band wagon. now they want no fishing zones, our representative, he says there's bushels of wrecks all right through the channel, well all the trawlers have to keep away from them, well that's as good as having a little area what's not touched isn't it; all them areas where you can't go for wrecks. All through here there's more wrecks than anywhere, all the trouble there was in the war all the shipping that went down. Then they keep all on about what's on the sea bed, like the fan coral and all this an' that. Well if it's anything to do with feeding the fish or enhancing the fisheries, then by all means let's have a talk about it. If you get's severe storms and then you get hell of a ground swell it's tearing all the sea bed up, they don't mention nothing about that, you know. I don't know, everyone seems to be on the band wagon against the fishermen to me."

DOUG WHITE

27ᵗʰ of December 1925

Family History

I was born at Tamarisk, it's just, actually at the bottom of Tamarisk Steps our yard was at the back of the little shop: there's one house at the bottom of Tamarisk Steps, then there's a little tea shop then a little passage up there and we lived up the passage, it was 3a Tamarisk Steps, that's where I was born. I think it was the 26th or something of December just after Christmas, 27th of December 1925.

I got something to do all the time, I still go to sea with me sons' but I don't do no work ashore: that's what happens when I come in here! I don't do no shore work. That's my pleasure now, making model boats.

Fishing Career

I can't think how I started fishing. I always wanted to be a fisherman. My dad and my two uncles and my grandfather was. I'm just building the last model of my grandfather's boat. This was, he had this built in nineteen, 'bout 1910 and she was named after my father: 'Young George.' What she done, he couldn't see for two or three years ahead and see, I built her exactly, bit rough to finish it, but I built it exactly under there how she was built and if you see, well perhaps you might not understand she can't swing a propeller, so she was never used because just as she was finished building, all the family got called up for the war, my father and my three uncles and my grandfather was on his own and he didn't understand, never heard talk of an engine but no sooner was she finished than engines come about. 'Course all his sons' were away, all my uncles and so of course he couldn't read nor write but he got in touch with the people from Glasgow that done the engines and they come down and took one look at the boat, a brand new boat, never been used but she couldn't swing a propeller. They didn't think, like they do now putting it right out through the sternpost there, they didn't think of that, that went under the quarter and see I put the quarter in there, my sons' understand it too she couldn't swing a propeller, brand new boat for the sons for when they come home from the war she laid there rest up 'til nineteen…well until they built the fishmarket there 'bout 1946, '47, '48. I just come home from the navy then and they broke her up then to remove all that lot up there and she never been used and that's all because they didn't realise about engines too much then and the mechanic that come down from Glasgow, I even know his name, don't make no odds now but he said to 'em she won't swing a propeller. He didn't know what he was talking about of course he didn't, but when one of the uncles come home he had to explain it to him like already explained to him in a letter from Glasgow and he went mad of course, got a brand new boat never been used, couldn't be used, she was a sailing boat, built for sails. The man who come down, he must have been from Kelvin, his name was Moorehead and somewheres we got the letter still up from the firm there, just turned round and said that she couldn't swing a propeller. They didn't know about putting it out through the sternpost like they do now, you only had to cut it in there in the sternpost and swing any size propellers she wanted but she was never used and I couldn't understand why granddad always chasing the kids out of it was playing in her. She was a big boat, one of the biggest boats ever built here and it must have upset 'em just a bit. My father went mad when he come home, he was the youngest in the family my father was, brand new boat that couldn't sail and couldn't swing a propeller. Sails was just going out, well 'bout 1915, but ah, it was rather a blow for the firm, of course it was. She was built about same time as 'The Enterprise', round about that period.

I started fishing nineteen… ah, well I left school at 1939, I couldn't stand the school no longer. I was quite clever, I went to one of the what they call central school, I could have gone to the grammar school but the uniform I think was a bit too expensive and I didn't want to go to the grammar school anyhow, I didn't want to go to the central school, I wanted to go to St. Mary's with the rest of the gang but I went to the central school. I was quite clever at school, didn't like the headmaster,

Left: Doug White (Doug's Grandfather), Right: Philip White (Doug's Father) outside the green netshop in Rock-a-Nore Road.

he was just a sort of piece whatever you call it; he didn't like me very much. Fishing was all I ever knew, was all I ever wanted to do and I was a pretty good fisherman while I was at it and, well still at it, I still go out with my sons' but I'm too old now.

Well I fished with my uncles' and my father but I joined the navy in 1942 and 'cause when I came home they'd all earnt enough money, tons of money, they was all retired. I bought a small boat off the fish salesman Jack Adams and Tom, I knew them because, I used to go and get the money every week, but I brought this small boat RX50, got pieces of her somewhere, now what was her name trying to think of her name now. She belonged, to Tom Adams, she was TA's, they always had a boat or two and I bought it, I believe I gave them £50 for it I'm not sure, which was quite a lot of money, it was nearly all my gratuity but she had two engines in, two Kelvin engines, and I began well, there was a new mode of fishing coming about

Doug White and RX37 'Bloodaxe'.

but I didn't have to spend a lot of time fishing, actually at sea and the fishing was just starting now, what we do now, the trammel net fishing and I done very well at it and had my boat built. We don't use her now, 'cause we had a small one. We gone right back to the fishing, when I started, when I first started but I done oh, about thirty or forty years trawling. I like trawling, gives you a bit more time at sea.

Well, I used to go trawling in this small boat, 'bout 1947 but I had a mate, he was the only one that was trammel netting at the time, his father, his family'd always done it and I thought, you know, it was a nice way of carrying on, you didn't have to spend long hours at sea. I like going to sea but you know, this way you only caught fine fish, you didn't catch no small fish and 'course things are altered now, there was about twenty trawlers then but now there's about three trawlers and twenty trammel net boats, 'cause it's easy, you've only got to go and shoot your nets and come back ashore and play, go to bed, do what you like and go and haul 'em next day, haul in. Yeah, most go trammel netting they don't do a lot of trawling they don't. They do go trawling occasionally, but it's mostly trammel netting, there's about two of them bigger boats are trammel netting might be three and the rest are all small boats they're not so expensive to run and you don't have to spend some time at sea like you used to have to. Well I expect now if we was going to sea trawling, I done no trawling for a long time we used to go and say four tins of oil on a trip, it was five gallons each trip in tins so it would be twenty gallons of diesel, I don't know what the price of diesel is, I don't have nothing to do with that part of it but it's a lot of money at the time the end of the week come and you want hundred gallon of diesel, expensive, see you all the week, well I don't know how much, I got no idea how much a gallon of diesel is now; my sons' do all that I don't have nothing to do with that.

I've always been interested in sails; we always had sails aboard the boat. I'm a bit upset now 'cause we've just took the 'Elizabeth' out to plant and I love the sailing part of it but I never actually went fishing with just mainly sail, I would have liked to have done. I always said I was born fifty years too late. I'd have liked to have been born perhaps even just before my father because he went fishing like he went with sails and it always appealed to me still does now.

A Long And Happy Marriage

Been married sixty years! I think it's sixty years next year, I can't remember dates very well. I'd earnt enough money to buy our own house. I live up High Street; right at the back: you can't see our house, it's quiet, you wouldn't know, it's as if we're out in the country where we live. On the high pavement, 110 and 111 and we're 110a at the back.

When we bought the house it cost us £800, and I had the money to pay for it, I'd saved it, I always been brought up to save 'cause fishing was always a funny business and we had the money, my missus like, to buy the house between us. We still live there. Well it was a lot of money, some of the money I wanted for me boat, but we had to wait a couple more years till I had enough money to buy me own; had my own 'Flying Fish' built.

Coast Guarding

Then I had me two boys Paul and Peter, Paul's the oldest one, he's known as 'Bud'. He got the M.B.E....yeah, he's got it for coast-guarding see, and my father was the local coast guard here after the war, auxiliary coast guard, not a real coast guard just an auxiliary see, and it was a good occupation for me when it was blowing we used to do what we called 'bad weather watch', so I got a living from that as well as fishing and so I was quite well off, you know considering how situations were. You won't believe this but I should say without telling too many lies, that me and you couldn't have sat in there talking like this in a telephone box at the end; that's all it was, a telephone box, and with a telephone. This area is big to what it was there was just a telephone in there and you could go in there if it was pouring hard of rain or anything like that but we used to keep a look out to sea occasionally see if anyone was in trouble and the local coast guard was Fairlight and the auxiliary was Hastings, was another auxiliary at Bexhill and that's all there is now, I don't think there's a coast guards station at Eastbourne, maybe, I don't know for sure but there's an auxiliary station there, and that's all there was auxiliary stations, there was, the next one from Fairlight was Pett Level. We didn't have a very big crew here, there was only three, my father, oh my younger brother, three of us but places like Bexhill and Pett Level, they're big companies of, must have been ten or dozen men I think, more than that probably, 'cause they were life savers as, you know, with pistols and this, that and the other. We got that latterly like, you know, but we didn't have that at the time. We used to bad weather watch, that's all we kept, I could carry on fishing without any bother because we only went to sea when the weather was fine, we didn't go to sea if there were gales of wind so it was a very good source of income for me.

It pays very well; we was paid well, and I've retired now from coast guarding, of course I have, but Bud's in charge he's the one in Hastings now, it's all more modern down there. They've got a coast guards station along here and there's about ten of 'em in the auxiliary crew, it was nothing like what we was in, you know it was just a ramshackle, all we done was kept a look out locally but they paid us well, to me it was much more money there, and I was fishing and the best of it was, you know, you only got it once every fortnight so we usually got money from the coast guard when we was earning money going to sea as well so, I done very well. I earnt enough; when the 'Flying Fish' was built she cost a few thousand pounds when she was built. She was built after the war probably about 1950-51 probably.

[There is a property at 13 Rock-a-Nore Road which belongs to Doug Whites' family, in the course of conversation it was revealed by Doug that it used to belong to his grandparents and was left to his younger brother who in turn left it to Dougs son Peter. The reason this came up in the conversation was that PB was aware that there was a 1914 cine clip in the museum which included a shot of the net shop that still exists in front of the house. The film includes a shot of Doug (we think) as a little boy with either his Dad or Granddad. There was also a conversation about the various branches of the White family.]

We were no relation at all to "Weasel" White, as silly as it sounds and there's probably more Whites out there, and though we're not related they're the same name but different. I can't remember; there was Whites lived at the bottom of Tamarisk steps, in fact next door to us but really there's, I don't know what number theirs was, really it was 3a 'cause it was counted up Tamarisk steps it wasn't counted at the back entrance what we always used and then they was White and I know we wasn't any relation to them. No problem with it, he's alright there was no problem they called him 'Queerwack' but I don't know why he was. There was a lot of nicknames, yeah 'Whiskers'', was my grandfathers' eldest sons' name and so was my grandfather, I can't think what my dads' name was, 'Wooz', 'Woozler'? He was 'Wooz', my other uncle was 'Pet' he was a 'pet' he was the loveliest man ever born. My grandfather was 'Hadlow'. Whiskers, he was my eldest uncle, he went to New Zealand, but his Dad wanted him back, he was the skipper in the firm and he wanted him to take the boat. He's got three boys, as far as I know they are still all alive, bloody great men, I'm a tiny little bloke next to them. Broke their Dads' heart they did when they joined the Army instead of the Navy, and they both ended up as Regimental Sergeant Majors, two lovely men. You would never know, you know, they didn't shout and holler, but they done their time in the Army. To tell the truth I haven't seen the youngest one about lately, Norman, he was only a few years older than me but the others were older, he was the youngest.

My boys always wanted to go fishing, we still go fishing together and it's easy life when you know how to work it. We don't kill ourselves going to sea now, but we've got other income see coming in from, not me now, but they're both in the coast guard service see and they don't do no bad weather watching like we used to but they're in the regular crew, my eldest son's in charge of it so…They are both beach wardens. Oh they're pretty well in everywheres. Well they're pretty well known especially Ginger the youngest one, he's a bit of a bugger. The eldest one tells me off but keeps me under trim. I have to do as I'm told but Ginger's lovely, he's a bit of a bugger but he's a lovely bloke.

I've enjoyed every single minute of my life, I still enjoy it now, I'm 84 years old and I still go to sea, I like doing it and I like playing with models. It's been my whole life. At the moment the wife's not very well but she's a year older than me, she's 85. Yeah we've been married for 60 odd years we haven't quite got 60 up yet.

Lifeboat

I was second coxswain in the lifeboat for twenty years. That's how I lost a bit of contact with the coast guard service because I wanted to go lifeboat then. I don't know how long I was in it, bloody long time. Joe Martin was the coxswain part of the time, Jack Edmunds was the coxswain before that and I went with the coxswain before that, Bill Muggridge, I think. Jack Edmunds was the coxswain most of the time that I was there, I wasn't there with any other coxswain, only with Joe Martin and I was the second coxswain with Joe for a long time, we were bosom pals we were, I don't know what happened to him, he went a little bit, well he committed suicide. It was a bit of a shame never seen him miserable or anything like that, I don't really know what happened there, bit of a tragedy really. I think that he didn't have a very good life with his father, I must admit that, he had to do as he was told. His father was training him up for the lifeboat and he went in a bit of dread of his father. He was never bosom pals with his father like I was with mine. In fact if he could see his father coming he's get out the way quick and, but his father wan't the best of…he was a big man, terrible big man, but I always got on alright with him no problems at all and I mean I used to spend a lot of time round his house and that but most people couldn't get on with him, although he worked along there with the anglers and he was in charge of all the anglers but most of 'em hated the sight of 'im but he kept them under control, that was his job but he was the lifeboat all his life; he was the mechanic in the lifeboat, well so was Joe till he was made coxswain, though I don't think it really suited him too much, he didn't seem sort of particular to be coxswain as he was to be the motor mechanic but we got on alright together and I don't know why, whatever happened in the end I don't, he never ever mentioned that kind of thing to me.

MARK WOODLEY

30ᵗʰ of July 1961

Family History

I went to school at The Downs High I think it was called in them days. Downs, Downs High yeah, which is in Bexhill. I was there 'til I was 15 and then I didn't bother going back the last year. I didn't like school, and I was fishing at the time any ways an', and I knew what I wanted to do so I didn't really see much point in going back to do my exams and such like because I wasn't very good at it anyway so, I sort of ducked and dived and got a few letters sent to the school and home, I think they give up on me in the end and let me run me own course.

Fishing Career

Well, I've always been fishing since I was a nipper. I used to go down the beach years ago and there was a couple of fishermen at Galley Hill that I used to go out and some at Bexhill and I just got hooked really and I knew that's what I wanted to do, and I just carried it on until such time I left school and I was very friendly with a fisherman from here Simmo, his son. I went to school with him sort of last year that I was in school I was with him, we became quite good friends and his dad bought us a boat when we eventually left school properly and we fished together but he wan't really into fishing same way I was and he packed up and I think he went to car spraying or something like that and in the end he moved to Australia and I carried on with the fishing and that's sort of the beginning of my full time career: and then I just, I went from boat to boat. I fished all over the place after that. I went to Rye: I fished with Mick Sharpe, I done about a year with him. I fished with Stan Pepper: I might have done two years with him. Chris Austin, I worked for him.

The first boat that was bought for us, think it was called Lorna, NN113 I think it was. Simmo bought it for his son and as I say that didn't really work out so then he sold it and a few years later: funny thing was I actually bought it back! I bought it from Rye and I had a spell on me own in that. I think I might have had a year in it and then I sold it and then I went back to Rye and fished out of there and then I bought: what did I buy then? Then I bought the RX204 from Eastbourne somebody had bought it from Hastings, Mick Pratt I think he was, was the person I bought it from. Then I took that to along Cooden there and I fished it there for a couple of years. I had quite a lot of trouble with it. I sunk it one time, literally. Well I was, in actual fact it was the first day I bought it, now I come to think about it. 'Cause I was buying from Eastbourne and I was, 'cause I was young and I was keen and I wanted to get it home, and we had nets down off Bexhill there and it'd been blowing really hard and as I kept going up to Eastbourne to pick the boat up and it was very calm at Eastbourne where it's sheltered round at Beachy Head and they kept saying, "Na, you can't take it 'cause you know you'll get to Bexhill and it'll be bloody horrible.": and so yeah I kept putting it back but in the end I thought no I'm gonna bring it home. So away we come, and we come down to Bexhill and we had a bit of trouble with the pumps and such like and we just couldn't clear the water in the end and I managed to get close to the shore and we actually came ashore at Cooden Beach hotel, 'cause I see a friend of mine who was doing beach work there he was driving a highmack and he pulled me out the water and we seized the engine up and everything it was a nightmare, absolute nightmare. I can't remember what the, the final bill was but that was one lesson I learnt the hard way that was, that was my first trip, in me first big boat as such and it, well it was just a bloody nightmare.

I dunno why I wanted to go fishing, it's just, there's just something in ya I think, it's one of them jobs, you either love it or you hate it and I loved it and I can remember when I was 10 years old sitting up Galley Hill and watching the boats from Hastings steam up thinking, "Now, that's what I want to do. I know I want one of them boats." I have really enjoyed it I have, up until the last, I'd say probably three, four years you know, I loved it I did, but I don't now and I can say that with hand on me heart. It's just not the job it was. I've earnt money, I've earnt quite a lot of money at times at fishing but I was never gonna be rich whatever happened, but you know you just not your own boss anymore, you're just under so many restrictions and it's horrible, it's just not the same as it used to be. You know the idea of fishing, I mean part of the job was, you know, if you wanted to go and earn more money then you go, you know you'd pull more nets in and if you want a bit more of an easier time then you had it you know, you could do what you wanted to do. I mean obviously you gotta pay your bills at home, but you know everybody's different you know, some fishermen have earnt a lot of money, you know 'cause that's what they do but I've never been that way inclined, as long as I've got home and everything else, I've always been happy, money's never driven me to sea it's just fishing that's driven me to sea and I did love it love but as I say in the past sort of three or four years it's just got ridiculous, I mean if we played by the rules you could not earn a living, you could not make a living now, there's no doubt about it and it's a shame 'cause, you know, there should be young people coming in to the industry and they're not.

Yeah, I got a step son and I mean, I'd love him to come fishing but he did come fishing with me a couple of weeks ago, just had a couple of trips, 'cause he's gone on holiday and wanted to earn a bit of spending money but I wouldn't let him, I mean I like him coming for the odd trip and that and it's nice to come but he's chosen another route now anyway, he's into forestry and he's doing really well, I mean he's in his last year at college and he's got a job when he finishes college and, and the money's fantastic. It's unbelievable, I mean the money they earn is, I mean don't get me wrong he's got like a credit card holder and it is thick with little credit cards certificates and such that he's had to pass you know and I'm so proud of him, I'm absolutely made up with him. I mean he's 18 he's still at college and when he goes to work he's on £70 a day and when he finishes college he'll be on £100 a day and I just think what the bloody hell do you want to come around here for and he enjoys it and it's a nice job, it's outside, you know, best of luck to him. When I got the 'Oliver Henry' the plan was really for him to have it but not now, no way. Oh it was fantastic, when we had her named here one of the best days of my life I think really, it was, I mean it's every fisherman's dream to have a brand new boat. That's the top of the tree as such, you know I mean some fishermen have had several but that's the only one I've ever had, only one I'll ever have.

Yes I mean it's, the way it turned out it's probably the worst thing I ever done; but you know I didn't know that at the time obviously, but well it was the worst thing I've done because obviously I had a mortgage on it and it's well it's been a bloody struggle make no mistake about that. Well I would think of selling it and packing it in, but what d'ya do, I mean you know I'm 50 this year you know, a couple of my friends are trying to get on the cable ships and I mean they've spent I dunno, nearly £3000 on tickets to get on these cable ships and they've applied for God knows how

From left to right: Steve Barrow, Mark Woodley and Admiral the Lord Boyce, Warden of the Cinque Ports at the christening of the 'Oliver Henry'.

many jobs and they all say the same thing "We want experience." and all this lot out here counts for nothing you know, being a fisherman for 30 years it's nothing, doesn't count for anything, which I find unbelievable but you know, it's very hard, I mean there's just no work about not that I'd wanna do anything else really. We just need to be left alone; we don't need quotas, we just don't need quotas whatsoever. The actual fish in the sea is our quotas you know, what we catch it's a drop in the ocean, you know, it literally is a drop in the ocean to what these big boats can catch and we're never ever gonna empty the sea out we're never gonna to take the stocks away it's just hideous, absolutely hideous. I mean for example this month we're on 50 kilo of cod well I mean, that would take me two or three hours and that's what we're allowed to catch for a month you know, and people sit up in an office up in London and say "Well you go and catch sole you got a bit."; there's no soles, you know you don't catch soles at this time of year: plaice, you might get a few plaice but they're very thin so they're worthless so you don't wanna catch them so what else do we do, you know that's what we catch; we catch plaice, soles and cod. It's just a no brainer innit, it's just a no brainer.

Well I mean we've said this for the last couple of years, I think we're very resilient, fishermen, you know we really are, we just get by, I don't know how we do it, I've actually sat down of a night you know, and worked out what's what and I just, and I don't think I slept that night, so I don't want to do that again. I'll just take each week as it comes and when we have a good week it's all very nice but it's not the same now because I know that's just squaring me up for like the last month you know. I used to ring up for diesel and order diesel and just pay for it but now you have to put it on a credit card and pay it off you know, in instalments. It's worrying times, well I think it is.

I don't know if it will improve in my lifetime, I don't think so. I think there'll always be some fishing, but the likes of meself and you know, like Kevin Bollon, Darren Coglan, I think they'll be gone I really do, you might have the Adams' there, I think you'll always have someone there from the Adams' and their family. Jason's not that much younger than me and I know his boys are definitely not going into it without a doubt so yeah I mean you say that as long as there is fish there will probably be fishermen but you got Podgy Ball, he's another one, you know his son he's going to college he don't really want him to go fishing; he has gone fishing but whether he takes it up or not I don't know.

They want their money then they're up the road and, no they've got no heart in fishing none whatsoever, not to what we had in, you know, and I wasn't the only, I mean there was, you know, there's lots of people round my sort of age you know all the same, Kevin, Darren, Marky Ball, Robert Ball you know you couldn't wait to get up in the morning to get out there and have some more of it, you just couldn't wait you know and well we did catch more fish, I suppose in them days.

Well I don't think the government want us here that's obvious innit, they don't want us here, I don't care what anyone says they don't want us here and that's all there is to it. We're the last ones, you know, they've gone through the big boats, the medium boats and the you're over ten metre boats and now we're the last lot, the under ten metre section and I really believe they don't want us here. I mean they can't do. They got rid of how many thousand miners just about overnight so they're not going to worry about a few thousand fishermen, and I just think it's just a crying shame, I really do. I really do 'cause I mean what would happen to Hastings without that, it'd be nothing wouldn't it? It'd be an own goal wouldn't it, an own goal. And I just think it's a criminal shame, but it's gonna happen I don't think there's any doubt about it. Like you say once my generation's gone, who's gonna take it over? There's no one, there's no one.

I mean we was up the pub and jarring it up and out at night clubs and all the rest of it but we got up for work, you know, these herberts nowadays they, you know you dread 'em if they go in the pub 'cause you know full well they aint gonna turn up the next day, and that's just how it is and it's just the way it's gone, I mean you can count the young people under say, even under 30 on one hand over the beach there can't ya?

I didn't read it but there was an article in the Fisher News just last week, one Scottish boat had 750 boxes of cod for one haul, for four hours fishing, 750, that's more than this beach will catch all winter, a whole beach! Where's the sense in that? It's gone mad innit, it's just gone absolutely mad. There's another example, last summer, there was a new boat built in Scotland when on his maiden trip, in his first trip, I dunno how long he was fishing for but it was only a matter of hours, it wan't days, it was days getting to where he was and to get him back home again. On his maiden trip he made a million pound on mackerel and in the same page there's a little article at the bottom of it and there's a man there of 55, who goes mackereling in Wales I think it is, somewhere in Wales I think it was, handlining for mackerel and they just stopped him 'cause he didn't have no quota. I mean Christ's sake what is going on.

I mean you know, you meet people that have got no idea about fishing, I do it all the time you know, they say "What d'ya do?" "I'm a fisherman." Straight away they're interested you know, you start telling them some of the stories and they look at you as if you've come from f*****g Mars! They don't believe ya you know because it is unbelievable innit, it is unbelievable what's going on out here now. It's just, I mean it proved it the other day when we was chucking all that Cottage man, that's what I call him because I never remember his name but it's our plight is just not publicised enough I don't think, you know, we're a nation where we sort of roll over don't we and let them do it don't we. We moan about it up the tea shop or up the pub or something but we don't actually do anything, do we?

Look at the French! It would never happen would it? It would never ever happen. I mean they must be under the same restrictions but they just don't take no notice of it, they take no notice of it whatsoever. And, you know I feel sometimes, well I feel quite strongly about it, you know, I mean really we should stand up and fight but it's very difficult innit and we do suffer for it, there's many a time we sit on the beach there and you know, mentioning no names, but boats either side of us they're coming in, you don't mind, and you sit back and you think Jesus Christ you know, what am I doing? What am I doing? And it shouldn't be like that, it shouldn't be like that. I mean I'd never ever you know, go and blow the whistle as such, I mean it's just something you wouldn't do. It does make you feel like it. You now if I'm at home and I look and I'm thinking how the f*****g hell am I going to pay me mortgage, and I've just seen him walk up the beach with you know, three or four hundred quids worth of fish that he shouldn't have got. You know I have to take my hat off to him you know fair play to ya, if you can do it, bloody do it. But we can't. It's another problem we given ourselves from what I see of it never ever worked out. You know we done all the fish accreditation, MSC, not worth the paper it's f*****g written on; absolute waste of time.

We had one trip round the corner, and fished right up inside for a few bass, thought there might be a few bass in there. Anyway, as it happens there was, nice big bass like five kilo bass, beautiful fish I can't really remember how many in number but I think we had about six or seven boxes and I worked out the price on what we actually got paid for it from two weeks before, and on one landing we lost I think it was £250 on just a lapse in the fish price: £250 in one day. How can you explain it? Because you tell me, you don't go in the shop and that goes up and down like that, so somewhere, someone has made £250 out of me in one day, out of one fisherman and it's, you know I don't understand it.

Well that's the trouble with fishing innit because we talk about this all the time, you know we go out there, we go fishing, we come in, we put the fish on the market and that's it and then whatever we get paid on the Friday, or whenever we get paid for it that's what we get you know, we don't have no communications no say in anything, you know, you wouldn't have that in any other trade would ya? I mean a farmer wouldn't sell his field if he didn't know what he was going to get for it would he? Know what I mean? In actual fact a farmer wouldn't even plant his field would he unless he knew what he was gonna get for it. You know and it's another kick in the teeth for us innit? Whereas all these big boats nowadays, I mean they virtually work their earnings out before they even land you know, you see it on the telly they've all got computers aboard there and dud, dud, dud, the fish buyer, fish sellers are sit out with email out all making this and all making that and they know what they've earnt before they've pulled into the harbour: and we don't know for a week. You know if we get hammered like that which, you know, I'm not the only one, it happens all the time, all year round, you know that's a right kick in the teeth that is innit?

Well 90% of our fish goes to Boulogne now, so we land our fish, land on the market, box it, grade it out, box it, put it in the boxes, I think the lorries from France come twice a week, it'll go on the lorry, weighted up at Boulogne market and then whatever it makes on that market, that's what we get. So it could be up there, the price could be up there or it could be down on the floor and I don't really know why Bolougne, I think it's probably the easiest way out. You know it's on a lorry bang and it's gone, we haven't got anybody as a salesman and we said this from the start. The trouble now is there's quite a few boats now that have left, you know, and they won't ever come back. So the fewer fish you get onto the market the harder it's going to be to get someone in there. The only thing you've got in favour with the French lorries, it comes off the French lorry at Dover and it goes along the coast and it's stop, stop, stop, stop all the fish, you know, right up to Poole I think, and then it comes back, stop, stop, stop, stop on the ferry and unload and so they will always be there, they'll always clear it up but that's all they'll do, they'll clear it up. You know and you got other fishermen on the beach here now that sell quite a bit themselves, you know to restaurants and such like but that's what we should be doing.

Without a doubt that was a sad day when the auction packed up, without a doubt. But it's not gonna come back so that's that. Perhaps somebody might start it up again, I really don't know. I mean something will have to happen on the market because it won't be able to carry on. I mean it's quite a big premises innit. I dunno what it costs to run it, you know, electric and all the rest of it but I don't know what sort of fish has gone though there this year but It must be, it must be losing thousands. I mean if you took the cuttle fish away from that market the actual turnover I should think it's pretty minimal. I mean Graham Coglan told me himself, I mean it's no secret, he earnt more this year in the cuttle season than his boat earnt for the whole financial year, the year before; and Paul was probably the same.

We got no pots, we haven't got any pots. It's another thing innit, it's a hell of an investment. You know to start from scratch you'd be looking at four, five grand I would of thought to splash out 'cause they do have blank years, you know if you splashed out yer five grand and had a blank year you'd be in trouble but they're a bit lucky that way in they get, you know, with all their surveys they get free nets and such like, so reallyall they need to do is their pots and that's all they do through the year, you know they mend their pots; I think Paul's doing it today. They don't make no nets like we do, you know but they got it a bit cushty, no doubt about that, but that's life innit. Well we can do it in nets, but obviously not like the pots 'cause once, you know, they put the pots out dun they and that's where they stay until the end of the season, they might come home and wash 'em out and put 'em back again but obviously it's a crab situation you know, if there's any crabs there, then obviously we can't put the nets there but they can put the pots there, it dun't effect 'em so they don't have that to worry about, that's another little bonus for 'em. But no I don't think cuttle fish'll save us anyway, that's for sure, it helps you along but it's a bigger picture than that I think. I don't know what the answer is, I really don't well, only other than to take us completely out the quotas, I just really feel we need to be, we don't need to be in quotas, I really don't.

I think we'd get, you know we'd go back to earning a decent bloody living; this chucking fish over the side is just, it's hideous innit, it's just bloody stupid, absolutely stupid. You know, when you're sitting on the beach and you're thinking of going to sea and then you think, "Oh f*****g hell if we get load of them we gotta chuck it back over the side!" automatically you're on a downer you know, it takes the buzz out of yer, and you need, you know, to be a successful fisherman you gotta get up in the morning and think "I can't wait to get out there!" And if you're not like that you know, you'll just fade away and die because you gotta have a buzz in yer to get you out there, 'cause it aint nice. When it's four o'clock in the morning or you've got to go off at one o'clock in the morning an' all that. If you're not keen you're not gonna do it are ya? And that's what I've seen over here now, you know, Kevin and Darren an' that, they've lost it, you know. I mean Kevin's boat sits up there, I think it's been sat there for two years you know it's £80,000 boat, you know, he should be going, but he can't be assed anymore, he's lost the buzz. He's been fishing all his life you know, it does get people like that dun it you know, I won't say depressed but it does get you down. I've been really peed off with it all.

RX427 'Oliver Henry'.

GLOSSARY

AREA 7D
Area that Hastings fishermen are allowed to fish in; it goes from Hythe Bay to the Isle of Wight across the Channel to the French coast.

BARRA
Dialect: 'Barrow'.

BILGE
In this booklet 'bilge' refers to the bilge pumps (see Brian Stent) and the part of the boat where any leakage collects (see Steve Barrow).

CAULKING
Waterproofing material used between the seams of the planks.

CARVEL BUILD
This is where the boat is built with the planks flush.

CLINKER BUILD
This is where the boat is built with the planks overlapping.

DAN
A buoy with a flag on top used to mark where nets have been put down.

DECCA
A company producing modern navigation systems.

DEES / DEEZE
A brick building for smoking fish

DEFRA
Department for Environment and Rural Affairs. They are the government body that sets the fishing quotas.

DOG
Jimmy uses this in a description concerning the flywheel.

DOLLY
A doll Fly; a trademark brand for a hackle-wrapped jig.

DRIFT FISHING
A type of fishing where the nets are shot and left to drift with the tide and the wind.

FIVE FINGERS
Nickname for starfish

GLENIFFER
A type of engine.

THE HARDS / THE HOLE
Fishing areas about three quarters of a mile off of Hastings (see John Barrow)

JINGLERS
Parts of a chain used for trawling.

KELVIN
A type of engine.

TO LAND
What the fishermen can bring ashore from their catch.

LANDY WIND
Northerly wind; blowing from the sea to land.

LISTER
A type of engine.

Lugger

The 'Enterprise' in the Hastings Fishermen's Museum is an example of a lugger. The name refers to the 'lug sail' used on these vessels. These are not used today.

Marine Stewardship Council

An organisation that certifies the sustainable operation of fisheries.

NUTFA

New Under Tens Fishermen's Association

Punts

Smaller fishing vessels ranging from 15 to 20 feet and undecked.

Otter Board

Used to keep the mouth of the net open on trawl nets.

Quota System

Quantity of fish a boat is allowed to land.

Railing

A way of fishing for mackerel.

Ricardo

A type of engine.

Seining

A type of fishing using a rectangular net called a seine, used generally for catching herrings.

Stemming

Movement against the tidal current.

Stune

Dialect: 'stone', weight, 14 pounds.

Swiney

Feeling faint.

TRAMMELLING

A type of fishing using a net in three sections; the two outer nets have large mesh and the inner has a fine mesh.

TRAWLING

A type of fishing using a conical net called a trawl that is dragged along the bottom of the sea.

WARPS

Trawling wires.